AIMR Conference Proceedings
Investment Counseling for Private Clients II

Proceedings of the AIMR seminar "Investment Counseling for Private Clients II"

November 9–10, 1999
Philadelphia, Pennsylvania

Jean L.P. Brunel, CFA
R.B. Davidson, III
Joel M. Dickson
Gregory R. Friedman
Leslie S. Kiefer, CFA
William R. Levy

James M. Poterba
Ivan Rudolph-Shabinsky, CFA
Karen W. Spero
David M. Stein
Eliot P. Williams, CFA, *moderator*

Edited by Dorothy C. Kelly, CFA

Association for Investment Management and Research

Dedicated to the Highest Standards of Ethics, Education, and Professional
Practice in Investment Management and Research.

AIMR Conference Proceedings (ISSN 1086-5055; USPS 013-739) is published four times a year in June, August, August, and December by the Association for Investment Management and Research, 560 Ray C. Hunt Drive, Charlottesville, Virginia 22903, U.S.A. This publication is designed to provide accurate and authoritative information with regard to the subject matter covered. It is sold with the understanding that the publisher is not engaged in rendering legal, accounting, or other professional services. If legal advice or other expert assistance is required, the services of a competent professional should be sought. Periodicals postage paid at the post office in Richmond, Virginia, and additional mailing offices.

Copies are mailed as a benefit of membership to CFA® charterholders. Subscriptions also are available at US$100 for one year. Address all circulation communications to AIMR Conference Proceedings, 560 Ray C. Hunt Drive, Charlottesville, Virginia 22903, U.S.A.; Phone 804-951-5499; Fax 804-951-5262. For change of address, send mailing label and new address six weeks in advance.

Postmaster: Send address changes to the Association for Investment Management and Research, P.O. Box 3668, Charlottesville, Virginia 22903.

ISBN 0-935015-57-4
Printed in the United States of America
August 2000

Editorial Staff

Roger S. Mitchell
Editor

Jaynee M. Dudley
Production Manager

Rebecca L. Bowman
Assistant Editor

Donna C. Hancock
Production Coordinator

Lois A. Carrier
Composition

Contents

Foreword

Providing investment counseling for private clients is one of the most complex endeavors in the investment profession. Meeting the diverse needs of individual clients requires investment managers to play a variety of roles—from psychologist/family counselor to portfolio manager. Success depends on being able to integrate these different functions effectively in order to attain the overarching goal of providing clients with the maximum aggregate return on their portfolios.

The professionals who undertake this challenge must not only be multifaceted in their skills but must be adept in them. Managers who cannot accurately assess client risk profiles and investment goals will not be able to serve their clients properly, no matter how great their mastery of portfolio management. Conversely, managers who have profound insight into their clients' psyches will not be able to help them achieve their goals without the investment acumen to craft an appropriate strategy. And even an appropriately chosen and well-constructed portfolio can prove insufficient if tax implications are not adequately taken into account.

The presentations in this proceedings show how investment managers can take practical steps in a variety of areas to enhance their services—and ultimately add value—for their clients. Whether stressing the importance of proper use of client questionnaires or the technical nuances of managing for after-tax return, the authors remain focused on the essential problem of achieving the highest level of performance for a given client portfolio. As a whole, they suggest that the key for investment managers striving to reach the ultimate goal of adding maximum value to a client's overall portfolio is to enhance each step of the investment process.

We would like to thank Eliot P. Williams, CFA, for his participation as moderator of this seminar, and we are grateful to all of the authors for their contributions to this book: Jean L.P. Brunel, CFA, First American Asset Management; Joel M. Dickson, The Vanguard Group, Inc.; Gregory R. Friedman, Windermere Investment Associates, Inc.; Leslie S. Kiefer, CFA, Bank of America Private Investments; James M. Poterba, Massachusetts Institute of Technology; Ivan Rudolph-Shabinsky, CFA, Sanford C. Bernstein & Company, Inc.; Karen W. Spero, Spero-Smith Investment Advisers, Inc.; David Stein, Parametic Portfolio Associates.

Katrina F. Sherrerd, CFA
Senior Vice President
Educational Products

Biographies

Jean L.P. Brunel, CFA, is chief investment officer of the High-Net-Worth Group at First American Asset Management. Previously, he held positions as CEO of Winter Capital Consulting, as an analyst and portfolio manager for J.P. Morgan & Company's asset management group, and as managing director and chief investment officer for J.P. Morgan's private banking group. Mr. Brunel is editor of the *Journal of Private Portfolio Management*. He is a graduate of École des Hautes Études Commerciales and holds an M.B.A. from Northwestern University.

Joel M. Dickson is a principal with The Vanguard Group, Inc. Prior to joining Vanguard, he served as a staff economist at the Federal Reserve Board. Mr. Dickson holds an A.B. from Washington University and a Ph.D. in economics from Stanford University.

Gregory R. Friedman is a principal at Windermere Investment Associates, Inc. Previously, he was director of investment strategy for Mellon Private Capital Management and held a number of management positions in Mellon's capital market department. Mr. Friedman holds a B.A. from Northwestern University and an M.B.A. from Duke University.

Leslie S. Kiefer, CFA, is a senior vice president and regional investment executive for Bank of America Private Investments. Her previous work experience includes management of both institutional and personal portfolios. Ms. Kiefer serves as chair of the Investment Management Marketing Committee and is a member of the Washington Society of Financial Analysts. She holds a B.A. from George Washington University and an M.B.A. from the University of Maryland.

James M. Poterba is Mitsui Professor of Economics at the Massachusetts Institute of Technology. He is also director of the Public Economics Research Program at the National Bureau of Economic Research and a fellow of the American Academy of Arts and Sciences and of the Econometric Society. Mr. Poterba is editor of the *Journal of Public Economics* and an advisor for the U.S. Congressional Budget Office. He holds a B.A. from Harvard University and a Ph.D. in economics from Oxford University.

Ivan Rudolph-Shabinsky, CFA, is senior portfolio manager at Sanford C. Bernstein & Company, Inc. He is also chairman of Bernstein's Canadian Fixed-Income Investment Policy Group and a member of the firm's U.S. Taxable Fixed-Income Group and Canadian Equity Investment Policy Group. Prior to joining Bernstein, Mr. Rudolph-Shabinsky was a management associate with AIG and an actuarial analyst with Kwasha Lipton. He holds a B.A. from Cornell University and an M.B.A. from Columbia University.

Karen W. Spero is founder and chair of Spero-Smith Investment Advisers, Inc. For the past four years, she has been named to *Worth Magazine*'s list of the best financial advisors in the United States, and she has been a financial commentator on both radio and television for more than 20 years. Ms. Spero is a past board member of the Institute of Certified Financial Planners and currently serves on the Editorial Advisory Board for the *Journal of Financial Planning*. She is a graduate of Lake Erie College in Painesville, Ohio, and is a member of its Board of Trustees.

David Stein is managing director and chief investment officer at Parametric Portfolio Associates. Previously, he held positions as director of investment research at GTE Investment Management Corporation, director of active equity strategies at The Vanguard Group, and director of quantitative portfolio management and research at IBM Retirement Funds. Mr. Stein holds M.S. and B.S. degrees from the University of Witwatersrand, South Africa, and a Ph.D. from Harvard University.

Overview: Investment Counseling for Private Clients II

Dorothy C. Kelly, CFA

Managing individual wealth poses particular challenges and is quite different from working with institutional clients. Rarely do private clients come with a mission statement or a well-thought-out investment policy. They often come laden with hidden biases and idiosyncrasies. Unlike institutional clients, they may have ill-defined goals or lack a comprehensive understanding of investment risks. Their portfolios may be poorly diversified, consisting of either low-cost-basis stock or stock to which they may have an emotional attachment.

In particular, for wealthy private clients, tax management is often the critical challenge that separates good managers from the rest. With nontaxable accounts, portfolio managers can devote themselves to issues of asset allocation, risk management, and security selection. For private clients, all of those issues must be dealt with in a framework that incorporates taxes—both current and future.

In the presentations in this proceedings, the authors not only offer insight into the complexities of serving the private client market, they also provide additional tools and techniques for helping managers develop appropriate investment policies to maximize their clients' after-tax returns.

Challenges of Private Clients

The job of uncovering investment goals and risk tolerances often falls to the portfolio manager, who frequently uses questionnaires and interviews to glean the client's real expectations. In their presentations, Leslie Kiefer and Karen Spero outline strategies for learning about a client's objectives and constraints and for developing a client's risk profile. The use of questionnaires has long been an accepted starting point for developing a client's investment policy, but as Spero reveals, questionnaires have limitations. To overcome the limitations, portfolio managers can use the information on a questionnaire as a basis for an in-depth conversation to draw the client out. Spero provides examples of questions that help managers uncover a client's real concerns and expectations. A discussion of different types of clients provides managers with insights regarding characteristics and tendencies that may not come out in the interview process.

Perhaps the most difficult aspect of the questionnaire and interview process is correctly identifying the client's risk profile. Leslie Kiefer explains how client perceptions of risk are often emotional, not rational, and thus are often misunderstood. Emotions can affect both client expectations and decisions in a variety of ways. For example, consider, as Kiefer does, the issue of tax sensitivity versus risk tolerance. Some clients are more averse to paying capital gains taxes than holding volatile assets. For them, the risk of seeing their asset base decrease because of volatility is more tolerable than the certainty of decreasing the asset base to pay capital gains taxes.

Given the incredible recent volatility of the technology sector, the issue of diversifying a highly concentrated portfolio has come to the forefront not only for managers but also for clients and potential clients who have seen their wealth rise and fall with the Nasdaq. Many of today's wealthy clients are wealthy in only one dimension—employer stock. David Stein's presentation on diversification of highly concentrated portfolios will captivate the attention of any investment manager working with a client laden with dot-com stock and/or options.

Once a manager successfully explains the role of diversification, the manager must evaluate the employer stock to determine the risk it holds for the portfolio. As Stein points out, some stocks may contribute significantly less volatility than others. As a result, some portfolios may benefit from retaining at least a portion of the original holdings. The next task is to devise a diversification strategy and implement that strategy, paying special attention to the issue of capital gains taxes. Restructuring a client's existing portfolio can be a significant challenge for portfolio managers; the critical task is attaining diversification in a manner that enhances the overall after-tax performance of the portfolio. Using a technique for mapping well-known solutions to nontaxable investment scenarios for application to taxable situations, Stein shows how managers can effectively identify the most efficient level of diversification for a given client.

Preserving Wealth

Two unavoidable factors that threaten individual wealth in the long term are inflation and taxes. Portfolio managers working with individual clients are constantly reminded of the erosive effect each has on client portfolios. Private client managers can use security selection and portfolio construction to limit the effect of taxes and inflation.

Introduced in the United States in 1997, Treasury inflation-protected securities (TIPS) are currently an underappreciated and perhaps overlooked investment opportunity. Even with the relatively tame inflation of the past decade, TIPS have a place within the private client's portfolio. Ivan Rudolph-Shabinsky writes about the role of TIPS in an asset allocation framework, in which low correlations make TIPS an extremely attractive alternative to other types of Treasury and fixed-income securities. The author also discusses the practical concerns of investing in the relatively immature TIPS market as well as the drawbacks associated with these securities.

Another often overlooked and poorly understood alternative for private investors is tax-efficient mutual funds. Joel Dickson presents a thoughtful discussion of this issue and how managers can evaluate mutual funds for tax efficiency. As the author points out, mutual funds can indeed be tax efficient, but evaluating the tax efficiency is much more complex than looking at turnover. A proper evaluation focuses on the fund's investment strategy, the character of portfolio holdings, turnover, accounting procedures, and shareholder activity. Mutual funds that use appropriate methods in these areas can be tax efficient, thereby maximizing their after-tax returns.

Jean Brunel provides an analytical framework for evaluating the tax efficiency of a manager's investment process. Security selection, portfolio construction, and risk management are critical dimensions that contribute to the tax efficiency of the investment process. In his discussion of portfolio construction, Brunel explains how an alpha-enabling transaction can limit taxes and generate alpha without changing the basic characteristics of the portfolio.

Evaluating and Managing Portfolios for the Future

In recent years, the desire for after-tax performance evaluation has increased among many investors, particularly those in the highest tax bracket. Many investors with short-term capital gains have become painfully aware of the taxes associated with those gains. Along with professionals in the investment industry, government regulators are noticing and responding to investor concerns, as evidenced by the U.S. SEC's recent efforts to require mutual funds to report after-tax performance numbers.

James Poterba addresses the issue of after-tax performance evaluation and points out that in some cases, reducing taxes can be easier and more financially rewarding for clients than generating additional alpha. He provides an in-depth look at the difference between pretax and after-tax returns, as well as a discussion of the AIMR-PPS algorithm for measuring after-tax performance.

Some wealthy individuals, such as Bill Gates and Warren Buffet, insist that they will leave most of their money to charity, not to their children. Even so, private client managers need to understand estate-planning tools and the complexities involved in managing multigenerational wealth. Gregory Friedman addresses the issue of multigenerational wealth and the methods for helping clients who wish to leave assets either to charity or to the next generation. Two commonly employed techniques for limiting estate taxes are the charitable remainder unit trust (CRUT) and the grantor retained annuity trust (GRAT). As Friedman shows, combining estate-planning techniques with proper asset allocation adds significant value for clients, no matter whether they are inclined to leave money to children or charity.

Conclusion

The presentations in this proceedings highlight the sometimes conflicting demands faced by investment professionals who work with private clients. On the one hand, they often have to account for clients' sensitivity to short-term results while attempting to educate them about the importance of long-term investing in general and the basic principles of investing in particular. On the other hand, as several of the authors emphasize, managers should never lose sight of the total *terminal* value of a client's portfolio, not merely annual performance relative to a limited benchmark. This proceedings offers techniques to aid investment managers in mastering both the strategic and interpersonal considerations of helping private clients achieve their investment goals.

Building a Client's Risk Profile: Working with Clients to Identify Risk

Leslie S. Kiefer, CFA
Regional Investment Executive
Bank of America Private Investments

Because investment professionals' perspectives of risk often differ from those of their clients, managers must develop techniques to identify how their clients actually perceive risk. Using a well-designed questionnaire and meaningful discussions, managers can glean enough information about a client's circumstances and attitudes to come up with an appropriate investment action plan. In designing optimal portfolios, however, managers must not only understand clients' risk tolerance, they must be aware of clients' emotional stake in their portfolios.

Risk in the stock market is a popular topic, but views on this subject vary greatly. For example, James Glassman and Kevin Hassett recently argued that the stock market is essentially without risk, while at the same time, Alan Greenspan expressed concern that the stock market had become too risky.[1] Many individual investors find the variety of opinions about risk confusing. A central role of investment managers is to help clients understand investment risk and how it affects their portfolios.

Bank of America Private Investments is dedicated to providing investment services for high-net-worth individuals, so what we do all day every day is help our clients understand their own attitudes about risk. Our investment policy process enables us to identify proper asset allocation guidelines, balance the trade-off between investment performance and taxes, and actively measure and manage risk. Such an approach provides the greatest potential for superior and consistent long-term capital appreciation, favorable pretax and after-tax investment returns, and flexibility in adapting to changes in clients' circumstances. This presentation discusses not only building a client's risk profile but also setting investment objectives and creating an optimal portfolio.

Client Perceptions of Risk

Investment managers talk about risk as volatility, a tendency that leads them to frame the discussion of risk in terms of the kinds of volatility that can be diversified away. Individual clients, however, are usually much less focused on volatility. Their perceptions of risk are often driven by emotions and, therefore, are easily misunderstood or ignored by managers who take a strictly rational approach to risk. In order to be successful, managers must identify how clients actually perceive risk.

Asymmetrical Attitude toward Risk. According to a VIP Forum survey on the preferences of affluent clients, clients were willing to pay up to 11 percent more for a portfolio that outperformed the benchmark but thought they should pay 32 percent less for a portfolio that underperformed the benchmark.[2] In other words, these clients gave managers almost three times as much blame for underperformance as they gave credit for outperformance. One caveat to this study is that 97 percent of the affluent individuals surveyed said that their current portfolios were outperforming the market. No wonder they did not give much credit for outperformance.

Clearly, an important implication of this survey is that clients have an asymmetrical attitude toward risk. Clients are particularly concerned about relative

---

[1]See James K. Glassman and Kevin Hassett, *Dow 36,000: The New Strategy for Profiting from the Coming Rise in the Stock Market* (New York: Times Business, 1999).

Editor's note: The joint Question and Answer session of Leslie S. Kiefer and Karen W. Spero follows Ms. Spero's presentation.

[2]The VIP Forum, "Voice of the Millionaire, Volume I" (Washington, DC: Corporate Executive Board, 1998).

---

versus absolute risk. That is, clients want relative outperformance on the upside but absolute performance on the downside. In general, individual clients do not care about relative performance when the market is going down. A key challenge for managers is to find a way to balance client perceptions of relative and absolute risk.

Individual investors also have a tendency to chase performance, although investment professionals know that consistent performance will lead to higher terminal wealth than will the same annualized returns if achieved in a very volatile way. Obviously, helping clients understand the benefits of steady but unspectacular performance is a critical task for managers.

Finally, with individual clients, the investment horizon and the evaluation horizon may not be the same. The investment horizon may be as long as 30–40 years, but the evaluation period for performance and risk can be short. For example, about six weeks after initiating an equity portfolio with us, one of our clients saw the value of her portfolio decrease substantially because of a market downturn. Suddenly, her horizon for measuring the risk that she was willing to undertake went from 30 years to six weeks. Such abrupt changes of heart happen all the time with individual investors.

How Clients Define Risk. Because clients rarely define risk in the same way that investment managers do, determining how clients actually define risk is vital. Seven types of risk tend to have particular significance for individual investors:

■ *Exclusion.* Exclusion is the risk of not being in the winning asset at the right time. Preoccupation with this type of risk drives much of client behavior. For example, some clients may feel pressure to have a portfolio that is virtually all Internet stocks.

■ *Loss.* Clients focus on the risk of loss. Every manager has experience with clients who say they want a 20 percent return with no downside risk. For individual clients, this type of risk is often much more important than relative performance risk.

■ *Regret.* Clients may feel regret no matter how good an investment decision has been. For example, they may regret having sold the stock of the company that their father worked for or that Aunt Mary gave them when they were 12 years old. Managers have to deal with the issue of regret in many forms.

■ *Cash flow.* Cash flow is another important area of risk. For example, many clients in the early 1980s who were fully invested in U.S. T-bills and money market accounts thought they had risk-free portfolios—only to see their cash flow suddenly decline by 75–80 percent. For them, the critical risk was not volatility of the asset value but volatility of the income stream.

One of my clients has about $17 million in Wal-Mart Stores stock and is wealthy by any standard. His family has owned the stock for a long time and is not concerned about volatility because they think Wal-Mart is a great company. Single-company risk does not worry them. This client, however, is concerned about whether he can meet his mortgage payment because Wal-Mart pays a very small dividend and the cash flow from his portfolio is only $68,000 a year. Someone worth $17 million is not inclined to live on $68,000 a year. He wants a boat and a big house. In effect, he defines risk in terms of cash flow, not volatility.

■ *Goal shortfall.* Many clients perceive goal shortfall as a worrisome risk. Managers must make certain their clients understand that the risk profile they set up for their accounts determines how likely they are to achieve their goals. Clients are often too conservative in identifying their risk tolerance and set themselves up for a fairly large probability of not meeting their goals for terminal wealth. At every stage of the process of building a risk profile, managers should discuss clients' ultimate goals and the risk of missing those goals.

■ *Performance risk.* Performance risk is the risk that the portfolio will not achieve the client's expected return. Investment managers face their own version of performance risk: The client will fire them if they do not perform. A frequent problem is that clients have portfolios with characteristics that do not match their performance expectations.

The Effects of Emotion

Money is an emotional subject. Because both circumstances and character shape clients' emotions about money, knowing a client's professional background or investment history can provide vital clues for measuring risk tolerance. Moreover, such information can determine the nature of the client–manager relationship. Managers must often manage emotions as well as money.

The easiest type of client to deal with is the "financial guardian." Such investors have inherited wealth and worked with trusted advisors before, so they have market experience and want to preserve and grow their wealth. Usually, managers develop easy, professional relationships with such clients.

A completely different type of client is the entrepreneur who has made money and, perhaps as a result of a liquidating or monetizing event, is in the position of managing money for the first time. Such clients are often impatient with financial markets and do not understand the risk–return trade-off. They often underestimate the downside risk of their stocks and have a hard time accepting that they cannot control day-to-day volatility in their portfolio. So, entrepreneurs require a lot more education about risk, a lot more handholding, and a lot more patience than most other clients.

Senior executives typically have assets concentrated in the company that employs them. During the 1990–97 period, U.S. corporate executives received more than $1 trillion in stock options—about 10 times more than during the 1982–90 period. Obviously, enormous wealth creation has occurred among such executives, and more important, their stock options may account for almost all of their wealth. Such clients frequently have no experience investing in financial markets.

The difference between old wealth and new wealth is significant. People with old wealth are usually less emotionally attached to the individual securities in their portfolios than people with new wealth are. Consequently, for people with new wealth, helping them change their investment strategy is often a matter of helping them make an emotional change. For example, 67 percent of senior executives say they have too much money tied up in the company for which they work, but when they exercise their options, 51 percent of them keep the stock.[3] Although they may understand the risk intellectually, they cannot overcome their sentimental attachment to the company.

Sentimental ties may be the least difficult emotion managers have to face. No matter how clients have come by their wealth, managers should never underestimate the power of greed and fear. One client of mine belonged to a family who had monetized a company and had thus come into sudden wealth. Our strategy was to invest for the future. The client told me that the family wanted a portfolio with strong and consistent growth and claimed that they could withstand any kind of volatility. To smooth out the risk, we planned to use dollar-cost averaging to invest a third of the money at a time. In August 1990, we invested the first third of the money—the day before Iraq invaded Kuwait. The stock market immediately went down, and the client quickly became concerned about volatility. The original plan was to invest the second third of the money right after Labor Day, but after the initial money was invested, the client wanted to abandon the plan. When the DJIA was at 2,200, we had a discussion about the pros and cons of investing, and he agreed to put the second third of the money to work if the DJIA decreased to

---

[3]The VIP Forum, "The Newly Wealthy" (Washington, DC: Corporate Executive Board, 1999).

1,700. Of course, the DJIA never got to 1,700, but it has since exceeded 10,000. We eventually invested the money—at a much later date with much higher prices. Even for this client, who had created a multi-billion dollar business and was a sophisticated person, greed and fear overruled rational behavior and led to an outcome that was not in his best long-term interests. As Adam Smith said, the stock market is an expensive place to learn who you are, which is a point that managers need to keep in mind.

Setting Goals and Objectives

A crucial role for investment professionals is helping clients identify their time horizons. Clients typically have goals such as building a portfolio to support retirement at a future date, managing retirement funds during retirement based on a certain life expectancy, or maintaining an estate to pass on to children. Knowing clients' horizons strictly as a function of time is meaningless without also understanding their goals because goals can have a dramatic influence on investment strategy.

I have a client worth $1 billion who has a family with 14 family members and who looks at time horizon differently from most clients. Based on the assumption that the average family member lives to age 85 and has 2.5 children, this client has made projections for the year 2140, at which time the family should have 725 members. Suddenly, a $1 billion fortune does not look so big. The standard measure of success for most people, which is a portfolio that outpaces inflation, is not good enough in this case, because a portfolio that merely keeps up with inflation will not provide enough money to support such a large family 140 years from now. A time horizon that extends to multiple generations is not unusual among individual investors. Think about how such a requirement affects the risk that the current generation should take in order to meet the goals for future generations.

To help us understand our clients' goals, we use the same method as most investment managers: a questionnaire. Our questionnaire is short and simple and consists of 15 questions. We have tested it extensively and are convinced that it captures the essence of what we need to know about the risk tolerance of our clients. We ask about their experience, their maximum downside, and their return expectations, and we let them set the level for international alternative investments.

Questionnaire software can use such information to generate a basic asset allocation for a prospective portfolio. For example, the optimizer might determine that a given client should invest 72 percent in stocks and 27 percent in fixed income. The program will also indicate that the after-tax expected standard deviation is 10.1 percent and the after-tax expected return is 6.7 percent. With this information, we can initiate a discussion with the client about the prospective portfolio and how it relates to their objectives for terminal wealth.

A graphic representation of such information can help the discussion with the client as shown in **Figure 1**. Panel A shows the expected return with income reinvested; Panel B shows the expected return based on growth of principal only. In both panels, the center line is the mean expected return and the other two lines show how a difference of plus or minus one standard deviation would affect the portfolio.

Given a market event of minus one standard deviation, the growth of principal, which is applicable to most of our clients who spend income, initially has a downward trend because the standard deviation is greater than the expected return. Early in the construction of the portfolio, we would talk to this client about the potential for loss and the fact that this particular portfolio would take more than 3 years to

exceed its beginning value. We would explain that in the worst case scenario, the portfolio value could be less than $6 million after 10 years. The key consideration is whether the client thinks this amount is satisfactory. If the client's objective is greater than $6 million, we would talk about the probabilities of achieving a higher goal. This approach is a good way to help clients understand how different market scenarios affect their portfolios.

Confirming the Profile

Once the risk profile is complete and the goals and objectives are defined, the next task, which is the toughest part of the process, is to convert this information into a real portfolio. Because managers discover the client's *true* risk tolerance during implementation, they should first take clients through a process of confirming the prospective portfolio. Key points to consider are determining tax sensitivity versus risk tolerance, evaluating risk in existing assets, and explaining strategies for portfolio building.

Figure 1. Expected Performance for a Prospective Portfolio

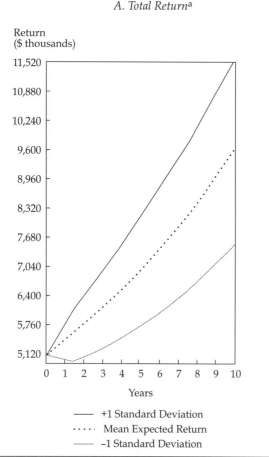

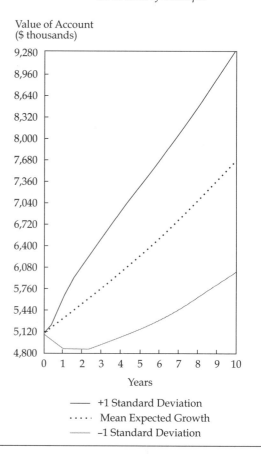

^aAll income reinvested.

[a]All income reinvested.

Tax Sensitivity versus Risk Tolerance. Some clients may prefer to keep a risky portfolio rather than pay capital gains taxes. They view such a trade-off as acceptable, although investment professionals struggle with the issue.

Consider a family who had two-thirds of their assets in Weyerhaeuser Company stock, which they had held for a very long time. They were comfortable with the stock's volatility. They owned it when it was $15 and when it was $70. They wanted to consider the retrospective possibilities, however, because they knew that Weyerhaeuser had underperformed the market over the past 10 years. So, they wanted to know what would have happened if they had sold Weyerhaeuser at the beginning of the period and reinvested the proceeds (minus capital gains taxes) into an S&P 500 index fund. Even though Weyerhaeuser had underperformed the S&P 500 during that 10-year period, the terminal wealth from holding on to Weyerhaeuser stock was greater. By selling the stock and paying the taxes in the beginning, the clients would have not only had less to reinvest, they also would have lost the compounding on the amount of money they paid in taxes.

For this client, the decision to accept the risk rather than pay the taxes felt right. In hindsight, the choice was correct, but the basis for the decision was the emotional attachment to the stock, not an analysis of the trade-off between a potentially superior return and the effect of taxes.

Evaluating Risk in Existing Assets. The next step is to evaluate the existing assets in the client's current portfolio. According to the VIP Forum's study on the newly wealthy, about 51 percent of the assets held by the affluent are nonliquid and nonfinancial. Managers have to account for such assets because they are part of the client's total risk picture.

Occasionally, portfolios are "locked up," which means they have single-stock issues. **Table 1** illustrates an example of such a portfolio. The cost bases are low relative to the market values, and changing this portfolio would entail substantial costs. The client does not consider this to be a risky portfolio because it contains the stocks of some great companies. As managers, however, we know the portfolio is risky. Furthermore, an asset allocation model indicates that this portfolio should hold 27 percent in municipal bonds. In order to change this portfolio, we must talk to the client about the trade-offs between the current portfolio and the optimal portfolio and explain the costs necessary to get to the optimal portfolio. Once the client understands these issues, we can discuss the strategies we plan to use to achieve the client's investment goals.

Table 1. Example of an Existing Client Portfolio

Shares	Company	Cost Basis	Market Value
8,000	General Electric Co.	$ 3,593	$ 926,000
3,000	Darden Restaurants	170	56,625
5,000	General Mills	1,353	401,565
2,500	Chevron Corp.	2,199	220,782
4,800	Exxon Mobil Corp.	2,494	345,600
7,000	J.P. Morgan & Co.	16,873	739,816
1,600	Hewlett-Packard Co.	22,032	132,400
	Total	$48,714	$2,822,788

Strategies for Portfolio Building. To help clients understand portfolio strategies, we have developed a software tool. "Risk Wizard" is Bank of America's proprietary Web-based interactive software program that helps us determine the risk in a prospective portfolio, and it serves as a great follow-up to the asset allocation conversation with our clients.

One of the primary characteristics measured by Risk Wizard is the tracking error for a given portfolio relative to the S&P 500 Index. For example, we can explain performance risk by showing that, although clients might expect their portfolio performance to closely track the S&P 500, the particular portfolio in Table 1 might underperform the benchmark by as much as 10 percent. Clients can also learn that tracking error is caused by stock concentrations. Risk Wizard, which shows the individual risk contribution of each stock in the portfolio, highlights the market weight, sector weight, and estimates of individual stock risk as computed by a statistical model provided to us by BARRA.

The software also displays the sector exposures of the portfolio. For example, this portfolio might be underweighted in technology by 22 percent. Given the performance of technology stocks over the past three years, such a portfolio probably has not met the client's expectations, even though the client may believe that the portfolio contains some great companies and has an acceptable risk profile.

The next step is to create a "what if" screen. For demonstration purposes, based on the risk contribution of each security in the portfolio, we can hypothetically sell some or all of certain securities, add securities, recalculate the tracking error, and show the client that we can change the portfolio from a 9.5 percent tracking error, which is unacceptably high risk in many cases, to a 500-basis-point tracking error by making the indicated transactions. We can also show the client how much the transactions will cost in terms of capital gains taxes. Thus, the "what if" discussion can lead to a discussion of trading risk for capital gains taxes, which helps the client decide what kind of performance risk he or she is willing to take.

The Investment Action Plan

Managers should understand the difference between making money and managing money. As a young portfolio manager who had just earned the right to use the CFA designation and who was intensively focused on modern portfolio theory, I managed a portfolio—or thought I did—for a member of the NYSE. The portfolio had only four stocks. In every meeting, I would talk to this person about diversification. Finally, he got fed up and said, "Young lady, nobody ever got rich from a diversified portfolio." He had a point. People usually get rich by building a company or concentrating their investments in a few highly successful assets. Once wealth is created, diversification can preserve it. An investment action plan makes this difference clear in regard to a particular portfolio for both the client and the manager.

The investment action plan, the culmination of our process of evaluating clients, is essentially equivalent to the "investment policy statement" in Karen Spero's presentation.[4] The investment action plan is a tool for the client and the portfolio manager, a working document that helps both manager and investor understand what the expectations are. The action plan sets a multiyear strategy for achieving the clients' goals, from diversification to risk reduction.

To make the action plan as easy to implement as possible, we provide a form for clients to fill out in which they simply check off boxes. The point is to enable both clients and portfolio managers to get all the information and come up with a plan of action to help clients realize their goals. We require our

---

[4] See Ms. Spero's presentation in this proceedings.

portfolio managers to perform an annual review of the investment action plan.

Conclusion

Building a client's risk profile should be an integral part, not a preliminary stage, of the process of setting goals and objectives. Because implementation reveals a client's true risk tolerance, determining the risk profile requires more than simply having clients fill out a questionnaire to determine their risk tolerance and then running an optimizer. Implementation involves managing clients' emotions and changing circumstances, and managers must be aware of the client's state of mind.

Managers should never forget that private clients are individuals and that the money they are managing belongs to their clients, who thus have a great emotional stake in the portfolio. As investment professionals, managers evaluate portfolios on an intellectual basis, and their role is to provide a quantitative, analytical perspective to educate clients, whose investment ideas tend to be emotional and intuitive. By helping clients understand investment risk and their own attitudes toward it, managers help clients achieve their goals.

The challenge is to talk to clients about risk in ways they understand, not only in terms of standard deviation and volatility. Managers, in turn, can learn what kinds of risk aversions actually drive their clients. Such an understanding enables managers to accomplish the ultimate goal, which is to design optimal portfolios that achieve investment objectives at a low cost.

Building a Client's Risk Profile: Using Questionnaires to Develop Investment Policy

Karen W. Spero
Chair
Spero-Smith Investment Advisers, Inc.

Questionnaires play an indispensable role in the process of developing client risk profiles and investment policies. The answers, however, are often unreliable because many clients are inexperienced or misinformed. To achieve the ultimate goal of client satisfaction, investment managers not only must avoid the pitfalls inherent in questionnaires, they must also understand that the information produced by questionnaires is only the beginning of a larger process, not an end in itself.

Developing an investment policy for clients based on a questionnaire is like putting together a puzzle. The questionnaire provides the investment manager with pieces of information to put together to create a complete picture of the client's needs. The process should culminate in the creation of an investment policy statement based on questionnaire answers, but unfortunately, questionnaires and, therefore, the resulting policy statements can pose problems. For example, although investment managers know they need questionnaires, they are not always sure how to use them. In particular, many managers are not sensitive to the subjectivity of the process. Questionnaires, in conjunction with lengthy conversations with the client at the beginning of the process, ultimately lead to crucial decisions that will set the boundaries for the portfolio.

The Importance of Questionnaires

Using questionnaires is more critical for individual investors than for institutional investors. Institutional investors are relatively sophisticated clients who have extensive collective experience and understand that the market has cycles. The representatives of the institutions also understand stated goals and objectives and, supposedly, have more patience than

individual investors. Institutional clients are usually willing to wait about three years for results. Individual clients, on the other hand, may stress the long-term nature of their goals and claim to have patience, but the average individual client will abandon ship within a year and a half if he or she does not get what is expected. So, the question is: What do they really expect?

David Dreman summed up the rationality, or lack thereof, of the personal investor:

> Modern economic theory is based on the assumption that people are rational and on what economists call utility theory. Investors consider the trade-off between risk and return and then spend, save, and invest their money to increase their overall return. Any adviser who has been in the business more than three months knows this is not necessarily the way things work.[1]

Many individual clients do not have reasonable expectations and often are not rational investors, which compromises the effectiveness of questionnaires. In some cases, investment managers may be better off not using questionnaires at all, especially if the client providing the answers is inexperienced or unsophisticated. Because questionnaires are the accepted method of creating investment policy, however, managers almost invariably use them.

Editor's note: The joint Question and Answer session of Leslie S. Kiefer and Karen W. Spero follows Ms. Spero's presentation.

[1]Mary Rowland, "Behavioral Finance: Breathing Life Into Rarefied Air," *Wealth Manager* (May/June 1999):70.

Advantages and Disadvantages of Questionnaires.

The use of questionnaires gives managers certain advantages. In practice, the answers provided on questionnaires are not nearly as important as the discussions that follow. Questionnaires provide a basis for in-depth conversations about the client's knowledge and background and provoke discussion about reasonable objectives. Managers entering into these conversations should have backup materials and charts to educate clients on what is reasonable and to quantify some of the clients' thoughts about objectives.

Because client objectives are not specific but general in nature, clients often need to be drawn out. For example, when discussing their objectives, many clients say not only that they want to get high returns but that they expect the investments to be safe and liquid as well. Except for those conflicting parameters, such clients will say they are happy to give managers freedom to do whatever they want with the portfolio. Clients seem to think that these requirements are reasonable because they do not understand the relationship between risk and return.

In the case of married clients, answers provided by clients may reveal inconsistencies in the thinking of both spouses. At Spero-Smith Investment Advisers, we ask the spouse to answer a separate questionnaire, because he or she often has a different response to many of the questions and we are trying to identify different emotional responses. One dominant person usually handles the money in the family, so without separate questionnaires, a situation frequently occurs in which one spouse provides the answers and the other simply agrees. One of our jobs is to draw out the other person to make sure that both points of view are recognized as important. Otherwise, the result will not be a policy that both spouses can live with. In some cases, the spouse who is not actively participating in the process might sabotage the plan by becoming impatient and seeking to overspend or by spending money that was earmarked for savings.

A perceptive investment manager may find a basis for compromise, even if spouses provide very different answers. For example, some answers might lead the manager to believe that a client's spouse is extremely conservative and wants the money to be in an all-cash position, but he or she might simply want something as specific as remodeling the house before investing any more money. Generally, one spouse is more concerned with the day-to-day experiences and costs of running a home. Perhaps the other spouse thinks only in terms of the future, reinvesting and reinvesting and never allowing any spending to occur. The manager's job is to make the spouses aware of their differences and to establish a policy on which both can agree. A compromise might include keeping a separate pool of money in short-term securities that can be used for certain types of spending. Once an understanding is established between the spouses, the focus can switch to the long-term policy that is so critical to client satisfaction.

The answers elicited by the questionnaire also tell managers how their clients will keep score. All investment managers need to know how their performance will be measured, and this subject is critical for anyone working with individual investors. Although clients might think they understand how to use indexes and benchmarks (and managers should initiate some discussion on this subject), they usually have some unspoken internal benchmark in mind that managers need to know about. If a client's unstated benchmark is the S&P 500 Index and the manager is investing in small-cap funds, the client is not going to be happy.

Although questionnaires have many advantages, managers should be aware of some disadvantages. One disadvantage of questionnaires is that clients may not understand the questions. Still worse is the possibility that clients may think they understand the questions and answer them according to a faulty understanding, a problem investment managers frequently encounter when asking about return expectations. At Spero-Smith, in the past, we asked about the expectation for annual returns after what we thought were a series of questions that would lead the client to be able to answer this question, but we found that the expected return was always higher than the answers to the previous questions indicated.

A second disadvantage is that using questionnaires assumes investors can predict their reaction to future events. Few people, however, know how they will react when the market has a downturn. How many of today's investors have even experienced a serious market decline? People who were invested in 1987 and withstood that drop (perhaps because they did not know what else to do) may think they have long-term horizons and can withstand high volatility, but even people who have experienced a market downturn may not accurately predict their future behavior. So, managers need to take particular care in exploring their clients' risk profiles.

Another disadvantage to questionnaires is that whereas the questions are "global" in nature, most individual investors compartmentalize their money; that is, they have different accounts for different purposes. For example, some clients expect education money to be invested in a way that is very different from the way their retirement money is handled. Questionnaires usually ask how long the money will be invested. The assumption is that all of the money is going to be handled in the same way. The reality is that clients often have a variety of objectives with multiple time horizons. Managers have to figure out how to help clients meet those objectives, whether or not they manage *all* of the client's money.

Types of Questions to Ask Clients. Managers should use questionnaires to probe clients for particular kinds of information and should avoid broad discussions about vague attitudes. Questions should be based on specific issues of central importance to investment policy, including the decision-making process, the client's patience level, the potential magnitude of portfolio decline, and goals and expectations. This section offers sample questions and suggests how managers can use these questions to gauge client expectations. These types of questions are not unique to our firm and are widely used in the investment management industry.

■ *How have you made investment decisions in the past?* Managers need to measure their clients' level of experience in order to determine how much education about the investment process may be necessary. Some clients may have never worked with an investment professional. Even if the clients have had brokerage accounts, they may not have used a broker for advice or the account might have been dormant. They may have had some experience with bankers, insurance agents, or financial planners, but more often than not, their accounts have accumulated randomly, often simply on the advice of friends, the most common source of investment advice.

■ *How long is your patience horizon?* Although clients' answers to this question are unreliable, managers should still ask. The best way to teach clients about the variance of returns is by showing them charts and graphs that illustrate long-term historical market performance.

■ *How long are you likely to stay with a strategy that is not working?* For people other than large-cap investors, this question has been a good test during the past few years. During this time, the issue of diversification has tested the patience of many people. Some clients may question why managers have investments in various kinds of securities rather than concentrating on the type that is currently successful. They do not see what is so difficult about this business, which makes keeping them on the right track a challenge.

■ *Why do you believe you could sustain a loss?* This question is extremely important. What in the clients' background or experience allows them to believe that if they have a significant but temporary loss in their portfolio, they will stick with the policy? Whatever

the clients' responses, managers should be wary of placing too much confidence in clients' ability to predict their actual behavior in the face of future losses.

■ *Have you ever sustained an investment loss in your portfolio equal to or greater than this percentage, and if so, what did you do?* Clients sometimes give themselves a lot of credit because they stayed in a particular stock despite the fact that it decreased to an extremely low point, whereas managers want to know to what extent the clients can accept loss in the *whole* portfolio. If the clients do quantify the potential loss, or if the manager requires a quantified answer, such as a 10 percent decline, a good follow-up question is whether the client believes a loss of such magnitude will occur. If the answer is no, then the manager should refer to a chart that shows, for example, a blended portfolio between fixed income and equities and the variability of returns over many years, not only the past several years.

■ *If your portfolio will eventually produce a long-term return that allows you to accomplish your goals, how much recovery time are you prepared to live with in the event of a temporary loss?* Harold Evensky raises this question in *Wealth Management,* which is a good source for getting a handle on how to quantify risk for clients.[2] Managers should frequently review portfolio goals with clients. Some people might say that goals are not worth discussing if they are being achieved or surpassed. If a client needs, say, an 8 percent return in order to retire at a certain time and the portfolio has achieved an excess return, then it should not matter if an annual goal is not met for a given year. The point of establishing a goal, however, is to use it as a tool to show clients that they are reaching their goals despite the variability of the market.

■ *What does success look like?* I often ask clients what they expect and what they think I can do for them that they cannot do for themselves or cannot do with whatever system or person they are already using. I also ask how I will know whether I am successfully meeting their expectations. The answer is subjective, but it can be quantified in dollars if you project the returns.

■ *How fast do you expect success to occur?* The typical answer to this question is five years or longer, but most clients are much less patient and become scared when they do not get their expected results more quickly. Some clients will leave a manager within less than a year if they think their portfolios are underperforming.

---

[2]Howard Evensky, *Wealth Management: The Financial Advisor's Guide to Investing and Managing Your Client Assets* (Chicago: Irwin Professional Publishing, 1997).

■ *What is your expectation for annual returns? What are your inflation expectations?* These questions must be asked together. Clients often do not understand the concept of real return. They say they want a 6–9 percent real return but do not understand the effect of inflation. Usually, even if the question is clearly worded to mean the return in excess of inflation, clients do not account for inflation in their answers. So, asking clients about their expectation for inflation is important.

■ *If we look back in five years, what would have needed to happen personally and financially in order for you to feel that our relationship had been successful?* When people are trying to project themselves into the future and deciding what their retirement is going to look like and what kinds of things they are going to do, the manager's role is to talk about what the cost of the family's current lifestyle is and what the cost of the retirement lifestyle probably will be. If the manager gets clients to think about what they actually will do in the future and how their lives will change, coming up with the right investment policy becomes much more manageable.

Characteristics of Different Types of Clients

Evaluating clients' personal situations in life, not merely their financial circumstances, is crucial. What are their needs and values? What is happening in their lives? What are their histories? Creating an effective investment policy statement is impossible without understanding the people behind the money. Four common types of clients—married clients, recently divorced clients, recently widowed clients, and small business owners—tend to present particular challenges for investment managers.

Married Clients. As mentioned earlier in this presentation, because certain things can happen that may cause a spouse to sabotage the investment policy, a manager must evaluate both spouses to determine what their experiences with money have been. Without antagonizing the primary client, the manager has to draw out the other person, cover what is important, and help the husband or wife understand where the other spouse is coming from. Establishing this understanding is crucial because fundamental attitudes about money and investing are often things that couples do not discuss with each other. People can be married 25 years and still not know how their spouse thinks about money. The challenge is to get both spouses to be more aware of each other's attitudes toward investing and to develop a plan that both can accept for the long term.

Recently Divorced Clients. Recently divorced clients often have no experience handling money and are uninformed, insecure, and extremely indecisive because they are afraid of making a wrong decision. Such clients have the attitude that "this is all there is and there is not going to be any more." They are terribly vulnerable and need a lot of time and hand-holding.

Managers need to be sure that they are ready to deal with such clients starting from square one. I have had clients who have received millions of dollars in a divorce settlement and do not know how to write a check. Such a situation takes patience, and managers who lack patience need to have someone on staff with an abundance of it. Such clients may have trouble making decisions, but deciding to come to an investment manager in an effort to find someone to trust is a big decision in itself.

Generally, recently divorced clients are uncertain about the future, especially if the ex-spouse owes them financial support. They may be worried about whether the ex-spouse will really pay alimony, or they might not be as worried about alimony as much as child support. Divorced clients often want to maintain their predivorce lifestyle, which probably will not be possible.

Many divorced clients are angry. The manager must make a good first impression and bring the client along slowly, which may well mean leaving money in a cash position for a longer period of time than is optimal and making sure that the client understands what is happening with regard to the different types of investments.

Recently Widowed Clients. Recently widowed clients often do not understand where their money came from or the current disposition of the money. They do not know what their life will be like or whether their standard of living will change. Such clients want to know if they will have enough to live on and tend to be consumed by small decisions that other clients could handle easily.

A client whose husband has recently died may not want to talk about the investment of the several million dollars she has received. Instead, her first priority may be whether she should keep the jewelry floater on her insurance policy and whether it is better to buy or lease a car. The focus of the discussion cannot shift to the client's large money issues until the manager takes care of the small money issues. Such clients need a manager with a lot of patience. A further complication is that these clients are overloaded by financial advice from everyone they know. The client's children might be speculating about all the money in the estate, which may push a client to consider an immediate gifting program to maintain family harmony. Sometimes the manager has to be the brake for such impulses—until an appropriate analysis has been completed.

Small Business Owners. With a small business owner, investment managers need to find out whether the client has a viable and transferable business or simply "owns a job." The difference is important because the investment manager will use a different strategy if the client has a business that will be sold or will provide continuing income to the client. Is the client going to need to create some funds that might be used in a buyout situation with an existing partner? How long will the money *really* be under management?

Entrepreneurs are usually risk takers, but a risk-taking attitude in business does not always extend to investing. The client may feel that he or she is taking enough risk in the business and thus is not interested in taking more risk in the portfolio. So, managers cannot assume that a business owner is an aggressive investor, because such a client may very well be conservative, probably with good reason. Thus, small business owners' wealth is often not bankable—that is, their own net worth is not so great after the business is subtracted, which is what a bank would do to evaluate the owner for a loan. Because managers want to make sure that their clients remain or become bankable, the investment policy may require a more conservative portfolio that can be collateralized.

A client who is a business owner is also under the influence of other managers, particularly accountants, who are often anxious to give advice on investing. Accountants are entering the investment business and seem eager to take over some of the role that investment managers have traditionally played. In addition, clients usually have business relationships with lawyers or others who may inject investment attitudes or advice into a situation. Because managers often find that clients have input coming from a variety of other professionals, managers need to develop relationships with these other people so that they do not sabotage the investment policy. Investment managers must know who else the client relies on or listens to for advice.

Investment Policy Statement

The culmination of the investment manager's process for evaluating clients is the investment policy statement. The investment policy statement has four main goals: to confirm portfolio objectives, protect the portfolio from *ad hoc* changes, maintain discipline for a long-term strategy, and restrain the manager or client from inappropriate short-term actions.[3]

Managers may need to include other provisions in the policy statement. Every investment manager knows to include in an investment policy such components as investment objectives, time horizon, liquidity, tax considerations, income requirements, and unique needs or preferences. The length and explicitness of the statement, however, depends on the type of client. For a client with little experience, the policy is likely to be a long narrative in which responses to different kinds of situations are included along with statements such as "you indicated that . . . ." Reminding clients that their own choices drive their investment policies is crucial.

The key is to know how much detail is necessary for a given client. The following is a partial list of items that supplement the basic goals of the investment policy:

- Establishing a spending policy. With institutional investors, the annual spending policy is usually known in advance and the policy derives from a tried-and-true investment decision-making process. With individuals, the annual spending policy is often unknown, particularly for clients who have acquired new wealth or are business owners. I have spent most of my professional life dealing with such clients and have experienced many spending surprises. Investment managers need to know how likely clients are to make withdrawals from their accounts, and they should explain to clients how such withdrawals will change the investment policy. Many clients maintain an investment in short-term bonds that can be liquidated for surprise situations.

- Making sure the client shares the manager's commitment to the strategy. Managers need to make clients understand that making sudden changes in their investment policy has consequences for the overall performance of their portfolio.

- Reaffirming assumed risks and creating boundaries for the manager. This consideration was particularly important during the late 1990s. A change, of course, is tempting when an investment strategy is not working well and the client is reacting emotionally to reports in the financial media. Clients might not understand, for example, why their whole portfolio has not been invested in Internet stocks. Managers should avoid trying to tune up portfolios and should follow the investment policy statement.

---

[3] See Charles D. Ellis, "Why Policy Matters," *Investment Policy: How to Win the Loser's Game* (Homewood, IL: Dow Jones-Irwin, 1985).

- Providing a standard of measurement. Establishing a particular benchmark or other standard of measuring performance is crucial. Not only should managers address this issue during preliminary discussions with clients, they should also formally define the benchmark in the investment policy statement. The goal is to avoid a situation in which the manager is criticized for failing to meet a standard that is inappropriate for a particular investment strategy.

Conclusion

Investment policy statements should be customized for each client; one size does not fit all. Designing a custom investment policy requires extensive discussions with clients, and questionnaires are the keys to stimulating and shaping the dialogue. Regardless of whether the policy is a long narrative or a one-page statement, it must meet the four main criteria: confirming portfolio objectives, protecting the portfolio from *ad hoc* changes, maintaining discipline for a long-term strategy, and restraining the manager or client from inappropriate short-term actions.

Drafting the statement is only part of the story. Managers should review the investment policy with clients annually to make sure the client and the manager agree that the goals have not changed and that no reason exists to change the allocation or the methodology being used to manage the account.

Question and Answer Session

Leslie S. Kiefer, CFA
Karen W. Spero

Question: When clients have counterproductive attitudes, such as the desire to compartmentalize their assets, is the better approach to show them the error of their ways or to work with their quirks?

Spero: You have to work with their quirks to some extent, but you also have to keep moving down the path that you want to travel. The solution is to educate them continually so that they begin to think more like you do and develop a reasonable approach to investing.

In the event that you have clients who want to compartmentalize their assets, you should initially agree. If you don't, you won't keep them as clients. If they think of a certain pot of money in a certain way, you're better off having that money in a separate portfolio, even if such an arrangement is more difficult to manage. To make sure a client is satisfied that we have taken care of particular needs or goals, we may maintain up to 5–7 different accounts.

Question: Given that building trust with new clients takes time, how do you manage return expectations when you may be the only advisor willing to tell clients that they shouldn't expect to win all the time?

Kiefer: Building trust is a tough challenge. Once, when I was on a sales call with a potential client who wanted 20 percent returns, I started to tell the client that this expectation was not rational, and the salesman kicked me under the table. Some managers tend to avoid telling clients the truth. At Bank of America, we ask our portfolio managers to discuss expectations with new clients

during the sales process and at least annually thereafter. Our asset allocation model explicitly states what our expectations are for the equity markets, the fixed-income markets, and each balanced investment objective that we have. Despite the availability of such information, some clients still wonder why the annual return in the model may be only 9 percent. We have to explain constantly that our return expectation is based on historical market performance as well as our expectations for the future. Such a conversation is not easy to have with clients, but we would do them a disservice by not having it.

Question: What are some of the most effective tools and products available for managing client expectations?

Spero: I view some of the available products with suspicion, but Ibbotson Associates' materials are helpful. We use Ibbotson's "Portfolio Strategist" software and use the "analyst" portion of the program.[1] The software provides historical data on disk that we then incorporate into our planning. If you use the allocation portion of the program, be careful with the client questionnaire and be sure you agree with its conclusions. The program creates a risk-tolerance profile based on client answers to five or six questions, but I found this portion to be too general for my purposes because it can't get to the essence of clients' real concerns. Obviously, I have much more information about a particular client than the computer

program does. You can modify the software, but if you customize each one, there does not seem to be any point to using the software for this particular purpose. Nevertheless, I recommend the product.

I do not like the optimization packages that are available. Using an optimization-type approach with an inexperienced client is risky. For example, many clients do not understand charts that show standard deviation; their eyes are on the high returns associated with a certain group of asset classes. Despite the shortcomings, an optimization package can be a helpful tool.

Ultimately, how you translate information for a client depends on the individual's capacity to understand it. A helpful book on the subject of dealing with client expectations is *The Management of Investment Decisions*.[2]

Question: When using historical returns, what historical periods are the most relevant?

Spero: I like to go back 40 years and demonstrate what the different returns might have been during that period of time. To look at trades only from the most recent past implies that recent conditions will continue, and you want to point out the years with negative returns that were not related to the 1929 crash or the Great Depression. You are better off saying these calamities could really happen and design the policy statement accordingly to keep people levelheaded. We use Andex Associates' Charts for American Investors for discussion purposes.

[1]Portfolio Strategist, ver. 7.1. Chicago, IL: Ibbotson Associates, 1995.

[2]Donald B. Trone, William R. Allbright, and Philip R. Taylor (Irwin Professional Publishers, 1995).

Kiefer: We use a chart that shows inflation and how each asset class (stocks, bonds, U.S. T-bills) performed in each decade since 1930. The chart is a good discussion tool for clients because it shows that, although stocks have clearly performed better than every other asset class in the past two decades, stocks did not always perform as well relative to other investments in earlier decades.

Question: Given the common perception that investing in an S&P 500 index fund is a low-risk strategy, how do you educate clients on the risk of a market-cap-weighted portfolio?

Kiefer: Performance is becoming more important for individual clients. According to some VIP forum studies, investors ranked performance only sixth or seventh in the criteria used to hire an investment manager, but in the past two years, performance has been the number one consideration. [3] Most of our clients don't understand performance, either relative or absolute, and managers need to do a better job of educating them. Clients nevertheless know to ask about performance, and they know that the S&P 500 has become a standard benchmark, which is a big educational hurdle for managers to overcome.

Investment managers often have a hard time talking clients out of index funds. We talk to our clients about the risk of owning only S&P 500 stocks. We tell them that they are going to own the losers as well as the winners and that we believe our equity decision-making process can separate the winners from the losers.

Looking at a market-cap-weighted index is interesting.

[3] The VIP Forum, "The Future of Advice" (Washington, DC: Corporate Executive Board, 1997) and The VIP Forum, "The New World Order" (Washington, DC: Corporate Executive Board, 1999).

Investment professionals have been taught to keep equal-weighted equities in a portfolio to avoid excessive risk in any one security, yet managers are being compared with an index that is cap weighted. If you're concerned about performance risk, you may want to be closer to a cap-weighted portfolio than an equal-weighted portfolio. The question of indexing is part of the discussion to have with clients in determining an acceptable risk level and expectations for performance.

Spero: With individual investors, because of the potential for confusion, including benchmarking in the investment policy statement is dangerous. We take out a lot of the benchmarking information because we don't think they fully understand it. We try to tell them what they need to know for their situation, as opposed to presenting numerous comparisons of different benchmarks. To take the focus off of return, we isolate their returns on bonds, equities, and cash; blending them all together does not always work because of the learning curve required for clients. In our quarterly meetings with clients, the last thing they usually bring up is a discussion of the portfolio itself, because they have other issues to talk about. The advantage of working with individual clients is that the challenges are more comprehensive than running an institutional account, in which you have no choice but to stick with the framework. With individual investors, you have the opportunity to educate them.

If clients choose the S&P 500 as their benchmark, then along with showing them what percentage of each sector they would own, show them a list of the names in the S&P 500. Point out some of the stocks they would own and how much of their portfolio would be invested in these stocks. They may not want

to own many of the stocks. Even if they don't care about the problems of managing a taxable account, you can point out some of the other problems with using an index-only approach. Some clients, however, will still want the index fund.

Question: Do your reports show performance relative to a benchmark, and how do you establish benchmarks for each client's portfolio?

Spero: Our quarterly reports do not show the benchmark. They show only the returns for an individual's portfolio. On an annual basis, we include whatever benchmarks have been set up in the policy statement. We don't stress the benchmark, but we explain underperformance. Outperformance, of course, is something we never have to explain—excess return is what clients pay us for (they would say)—but we certainly want them to be comfortable with their portfolio's underperformance because we hope that we are still meeting their goals.

Question: How do you get clients to open up about their assets other than those managed by your firm?

Spero: In the initial interview, you should explain why you need a complete picture of how they're managing their financial life. If they have assets that are not disclosed, they need to know how that nondisclosure can skew the decision-making process. Starting with questions about their motivations and expectations opens the door to a discussion of their experiences and money issues. People love to talk about themselves, so if you are quiet and listen, the "family tree" of their financial background will come out.

Question: How is the subject of risk different for private clients, as opposed to institutional clients?

Spero: Private clients define risk differently than institutional clients do. In my experience, the institutional client looks at risk relative only to a benchmark. The private client looks at factors that may not result from an analytical approach to money management but that may be personal and emotional.

Kiefer: Institutional clients are satisfied as long as a certain spending policy is met and as long as the trustees feel that you're following the policy statement. Private clients look at their portfolios constantly; they might want to use a lot of the money and thus care about what is going on with every single dollar.

Question: Do individual clients understand the quantitative measures of risk, such as standard deviation, and how do you uncover their feelings about risk if they have not experienced downturns?

Kiefer: You don't truly understand clients' attitudes toward risk until they've experienced a downturn, but it is incumbent upon managers to prepare their clients for a loss. Using terms such as standard deviation is not necessary. Most clients' eyes glaze over when they hear statistical jargon, and you lose them. Questions about how they would tolerate a loss for an extended period of time can help you get at their attitudes, but as everyone who manages money for individual clients has learned, you don't learn what their true risk tolerance is until they have suffered a loss of some kind.

Spero: Because clients don't understand standard deviation and other technical terms used by investment professionals, a lot of investment questionnaires are ineffective. If your client doesn't understand the questions, the questionnaire won't help you understand your client in the long run. Long, in-depth discussions are important. To whatever extent you want something in writing, you should make notes or diary entries so that you can continue to talk about the things they don't understand. Putting their goals in dollar amounts is also helpful.

Question: How do you adjust your process when another advisor (such as a financial consultant, accountant, or attorney) is involved and you manage only a portion of the assets?

Spero: Find out as soon as possible who the client has relationships with. Find out all the vital information, such as whom they trust and how long they have had these relationships. Whether at the first meeting or by the end of the first year, suggest having an annual meeting that includes the other advisors and the client. We have found such meetings to be helpful. The accountants particularly like being included in these discussions so that they know you're not doing things that will mess up the tax return, and the attorneys welcome the opportunity to have a reason to be in front of the client and the other players. If you can get them thinking in terms of working together toward common goals, the discussions will help you and may even cause you to change the way that you're managing the funds. Because you might not know about everything that is happening with the client, you need this kind of coordination among different advisors. If the client seems reluctant to introduce you, ask the client whether he or she minds if you call the other people. Usually, clients don't care as long as they don't get a bill, which may or may not happen, but establishing relationships goes a long way in avoiding sabotage by other parties.

Question: Would you provide more detail on diversification strategies, such as STARS (specialized term appreciation retention sales) and cashless collars?

Kiefer: Most of our clients, especially those with large, concentrated positions, don't want to pay taxes. A couple of years ago, one of the most popular diversification strategies was for clients to go short against the box. Most advisors to the affluent were aggressively using this strategy until Congress eliminated its tax advantages. Since then, we have looked for other ways to monetize a concentrated position without paying taxes.

A cashless collar and a loan is one strategy. We put a collar on the stock that is costless to execute—that is, the proceeds from the put and the call offset each other, and a certain percentage, usually a 10 percent swing either upside or downside, allows you not only to cushion the downside of the stock but also to cap the upside. Once we've collared the security, we can make a loan on it and then use a portion of the loan proceeds to develop a diversified portfolio.

The term "STARS" is proprietary, but the strategy is equivalent to a variable-share prepaid forward sale. The client sells the stock for a given price five years from now, and a portion of the proceeds from the sale is available immediately, thereby allowing the client to invest in a diversified portfolio. The method is called a variable-share sale because the proportion of the shares delivered varies with the value of the shares at expiration. If the security at the end of the five years is at its floor price, the client delivers 100 percent of the shares that were sold forward. If the price of the stock is above the floor price, then the client delivers a proportion of the shares. The client can reinvest the proceeds from this forward sale in marginable securities—unlike a loan against securities, in which regulatory issues and margin requirements limit the amount of proceeds that can be invested in securities.

Diversification of Highly Concentrated Portfolios in the Presence of Taxes

David M. Stein[1]
Managing Director and Chief Investment Officer
Parametric Portfolio Associates

Although taxes are an economic reality for most client portfolios, much of the academic financial literature deals with investment scenarios in the absence of taxes. The distinction is significant for investment managers because the presence of taxes complicates the diversification decision for clients with highly concentrated portfolios. To simplify the problem, managers can use a mathematical mapping technique to help determine the appropriate trade-off between taxes and diversification in order to maximize a client's terminal wealth.

This presentation addresses diversification in the presence of taxes. The focus is on a taxable investor who wants to diversify a concentrated holding in order to reduce risk of the portfolio. The challenge is to decide how much of the portfolio to diversify, given the certainty of paying taxes. Although this problem is simplified and idealized, it is an important type of problem for investment managers who deal with private investors and is at the heart of many more-complex problems that involve financial decision making in the presence of taxes.

Risk and Taxes

Consider an investor who has a great deal of wealth invested in a single concentrated holding—say, an executive who has $100 million in company stock at a zero-cost basis—and who would like to diversify. With a maximum long-term capital gains tax rate of 20 percent, the investor retains only 80 percent of anything sold. For simplicity, we will think of the diversified alternative as being invested in a benchmark that represents the market as a whole, such as the Wilshire 5000 Index, the Russell 3000 Index, or some other broadly defined universe.

The diversification decision will depend on the characteristics of the initial holding. If the concentrated holding is a young company that is likely to incur a huge amount of volatility, such as Micron Technology, the decision would differ from the case in which the holding is General Electric Company (GE), an established, large, diversified company with a solid, stable management and a history of earnings. Even less volatile would be an initial portfolio of 10 stocks. In each case, the decision would differ.

This presentation deals with two types of risk. The first type is "total risk," or the volatility (standard deviation of annual returns) of the portfolio. The second type is tracking error, which is a measure of how the portfolio differs from its benchmark. Although other notions of risk exist, such as value at risk, this presentation focuses only on volatility and tracking error.

Jean Brunel's presentation on tax-aware equity investing addresses the question of risk in the presence of taxes.[2] Taxes change risk in two ways. First, risk (as defined by volatility of return) changes because taxes reduce the upside as well as the downside. That is, taxes dampen volatility. An investor who is comfortable investing 60 percent in stocks and 40 percent in bonds for a tax-exempt portfolio ought to be willing to incur a higher level of risk, perhaps 70 percent stocks and 30 percent bonds, in a taxable

---

[1]This presentation is based on an article being developed jointly by David M. Stein, Premkumar Narasimhan, and Charles E. Appeadu of Parametric Associates and Andrew F. Siegel of the University of Washington. The paper, which has been submitted for publication, includes the mathematical formulation.

[2]See Mr. Brunel's presentation in this proceedings.

portfolio. Second, taxes change risk by putting a twist on the volatility. The U.S. tax code provides investors an option to defer the payment of taxes on capital gains, which can be thought of as a free loan, but to realize capital losses immediately. This option dampens the downside more than the upside.

In this example, the task is to work with the investor's end-of-period wealth after taxes, which is expressed as a probability distribution. The investor has, say, a 20-year horizon. The single-stock portfolio has a starting value of $1 (with zero-cost basis) and an annual expected return of 10 percent, of which dividends are 3 percent. Also, assume a lognormal stochastic process with annual volatility of 40 percent.

To put 40 percent volatility in context, the following are examples of levels of volatility over the 1994–99 period (1997–99 for America Online and Amazon.com):

S&P 500 Index	14%
Exxon Mobil Corporation	16
GE	21
IBM	30
Microsoft Corporation	35
Micron Technology	72
AOL	84
Amazon	124

Given the parameters described above, **Figure 1** shows the probability distribution of wealth after 20 years. The distribution has a very wide uncertainty. The expected value at the end of the 20 years is $4.40. The most likely value (the mode of the distribution) is only $0.50. The initial $1 is very likely to decrease in value. The likelihood of ending up with only $1 in 20 years is about 44 percent. At an inflation rate of 3.5 percent a year, the initial $1 investment doubles to $2 in 20 years. The chance of not keeping up with inflation is 62 percent. Although the expected return is high, the investor should clearly be very concerned with the effect of volatility.

In contrast, compare this distribution with a case in which the investor liquidates the concentrated holding, as shown in **Figure 2**. The investor sells the holding and invests the $0.80 remaining after taxes in the benchmark (market) average, which has a volatility of 15 percent. The investor can expect less than before, $3.70 compared with the previous $4.40. This difference is mainly a result of the initial tax cost. The distribution of final wealth, however, is now much less uncertain. The probability of having less than $1 in 20 years is only about 1 percent, and the probability of not keeping up with inflation is only about 20 percent.

An instructive comparison is to review a framework for addressing a similar diversification problem in the *absence* of taxes. **Figure 3** shows the risk–

Figure 1. After-Tax Liquidation Value for a Concentrated Portfolio with a 20-Year Horizon

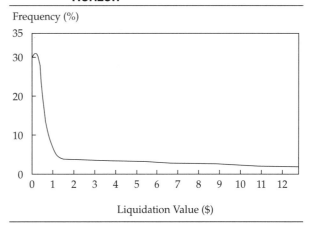

Figure 2. After-Tax Liquidation Value for a Diversified Portfolio with a 20-Year Horizon

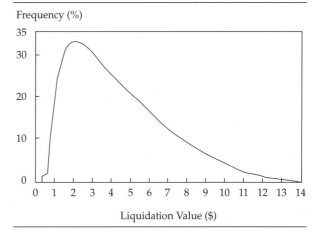

return trade-off between Asset 1, which is a diversified portfolio with lower return and lower risk, and Asset 2, which is the concentrated holding. There are many ways to choose a decision point, and a standard, easy approach is to seek the point on the curve that provides the maximum Sharpe ratio—that is, to maximize the excess return (return minus risk-free rate) divided by the excess volatility.

Figure 3 is not directly applicable to the taxable case for three reasons. First, taxes paid now are certain rather than uncertain. Second, the preferable approach is to think about the terminal wealth distribution rather than *annual* returns and risks, because for taxable investors, the horizon is a critical aspect of the analysis. Finally, taxes complicate cash flows, and the choice of whether to pay taxes now or at some point in the future changes the nature of the problem.

Figure 3. Risk–Return Trade-Off for a Tax-Exempt Portfolio

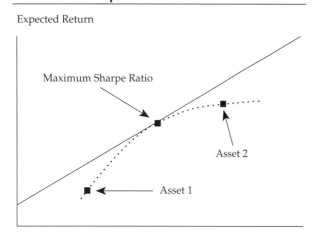

Although standard decision-making approaches exist for the tax-exempt case, no ready answer is available for the taxable case.

Diversification Problem I

The first diversification problem deals with total risk and diversifying a concentrated holding. This example uses the following parametric assumptions, many of which are not crucial:

- The initial cost basis is zero.
- The concentrated portfolio and the market benchmark have the same expected return of 10 percent.
- The volatility (standard deviation) of the concentrated holding is 25 percent and that of the market is 15 percent.
- The investment betas are both equal to 1.
- The horizon is 20 years.
- The uncertainty is expressed as a lognormal stochastic process.
- There are no dividends.
- The risk-free rate is 6 percent.
- Assets will be liquidated at the horizon.

The key to solving the diversification problem is to compute the joint distribution of the end-of-period wealth of the diversified position and the benchmark and then determine the annualized returns, risks, and covariances of this distribution and solve the *similar* pretax problem to determine the maximum Sharpe ratio. That is, transform the taxable end-of-period problem into a similar "tax-adjusted" problem by matching up the end-of-period distributions. The actual investor in the taxable world sells part of the initial concentrated portfolio, pays tax on the proceeds, uses the *net* proceeds to buy the benchmark,

and liquidates, paying tax at the end. The virtual investor in the tax-adjusted world sells part of the initial virtual asset, does *not* pay tax, uses the *full* proceeds to buy a virtual benchmark, and liquidates and pays tax at the horizon. Both investors get the same horizon distribution.

Figure 4 shows the problem in the tax-adjusted world. To maximize the Sharpe ratio, the investor with a concentrated holding with initial volatility of 25 percent (Portfolio A) would need to sell 86 percent of the holding. The numerical value of 86 percent depends on the assumptions, including any excess return expectation for the concentrated holding. Three other assumptions are also critical: volatility, horizon, and cost basis.

Figure 4. Risk–Return Trade-Off for a Taxable Portfolio

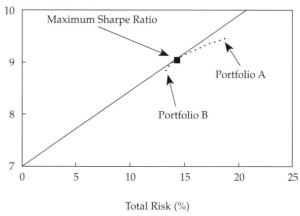

Note: Based on the following assumptions: expected return, 10 percent; benchmark volatility, 15 percent; initial volatility, 25 percent; portfolio beta, 1; tax rate, 20 percent; horizon, 20 years; risk-free rate, 6 percent; cost basis, 0 percent.

Volatility. In **Figure 5**, Panel A shows how the maximum Sharpe ratio decision changes as the volatility of the initial holding changes. Panel B shows how the diversification changes as a function of volatility. An asset with 40 percent volatility would require diversifying 96 percent of the portfolio. A stock with 20 percent volatility, such as GE, would require diversifying 65 percent. A relatively high level of diversification is recommended for most securities.

Horizon. The second key assumption is time horizon. In **Figure 6**, Panel A shows that, in general, the shorter the horizon, the less the portfolio should be diversified. The 86 percent recommendation drops to 80 percent if the security is to be held 10 years and rises to 90 percent if the horizon is 30 years. Panel B shows how diversification changes as a function of

Figure 5. Effect of Initial Stock Volatility on Diversification

A. Change in Maximum Sharpe Ratio

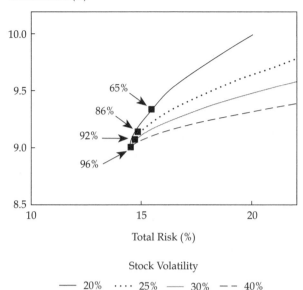

B. Change in Diversification Level

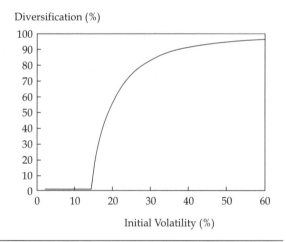

Note: Based on the following assumptions: expected return, 10 percent; benchmark volatility, 15 percent; initial volatility, 25 percent; portfolio beta, 1; tax rate, 20 percent; horizon, 20 years; risk-free rate, 6 percent; cost basis, 0 percent.

the horizon. A less volatile stock requires less diversification, if the horizon is short.

Cost Basis. Finally, the cost basis affects the level of diversification, as shown in **Figure 7**. Panel A shows that the lower the cost basis, the less the portfolio needs be diversified, and Panel B shows diversification as a function of cost basis. At a full-cost basis—that is, if the cost basis of the security is equal to the market value—the solution is to diversify

immediately: Under the assumption of equal expected returns, the investor has no reason to hold the concentrated stock.

Diversification Problem II

Thus far, we have addressed the mathematical problem of seeking low total volatility. A related problem— a common practical one—is that of paying taxes to reduce risk as measured by *tracking error* (standard deviation of excess return). Again, the challenge is to figure out how best to diversify the portfolio.

Figure 6. Effect of Horizon on Diversification

A. Change in Maximum Sharpe Ratio

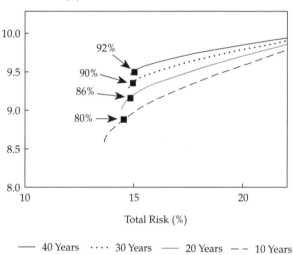

B. Change in Diversification Level

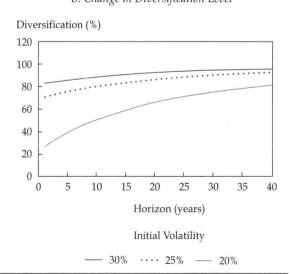

Note: Based on the following assumptions: expected return, 10 percent; benchmark volatility, 15 percent; beta, 1; tax rate, 20 percent; risk-free rate, 6 percent; cost basis, 0 percent.

Figure 7. Effect of Cost Basis on Diversification

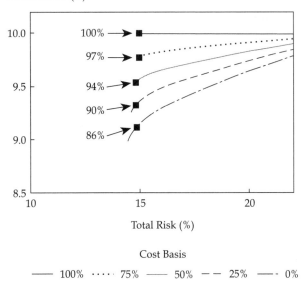

A. Change in Maximum Sharpe Ratio

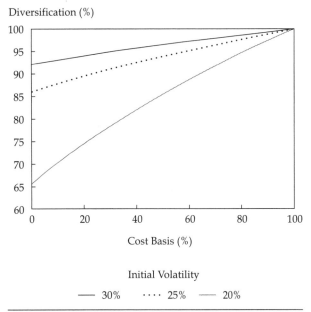

B. Change in Diversification Level

Note: Based on the following assumptions: expected return, 10 percent; benchmark volatility, 15 percent; beta, 1; tax rate, 20 percent; horizon, 20 years; risk-free rate, 6 percent.

Figure 8 shows such an empirical example. In this case, the investor has an initial portfolio of 10–20 securities that exhibits risks with respect to a target benchmark of about 7 percent. For this case, our approach is to use a quadratic optimization process to plot an empirical tracking-error-versus-tax-cost curve. At each level of tracking error, the process seeks the lowest possible tax cost. In this case, some relatively high-cost-basis holdings can be liquidated inexpensively and the cash raised can be used to reduce tracking. Paying taxes becomes necessary as we lower the risk of tracking error. In the extreme, getting to a perfectly tracking index portfolio would require taxes of 6 percent of the portfolio value.

For the general problem, the decision point on the curve depends on the investor's tolerance for tracking-error risk. Some investors do not want to incur tracking error, even at a high tax cost. Others are willing to incur a higher tracking error and are extremely reluctant to pay taxes.

Figure 9 shows a curve that represents a trade-off between excess return and tracking error in the *absence* of taxes. This problem is similar to the problem of choosing an investment manager, in which an expectation of excess return comes at a cost of tracking risk. The choice depends on the confidence in the alpha. If the expected return is 50 basis points (bps) a year but the cost is 400 bps in tracking error, the trade-off is poor. On the other hand, a tracking error risk of 4 percent with an expected return of 200 bps is more appealing. A simple measurement criterion is the information ratio—that is, the ratio of excess return to tracking-error risk.

To find a decision point for this problem, adapt it to a tax-exempt formulation (similar to the approach used for the first diversification problem). In this case, at Parametric, our decision about how much of the portfolio to diversify and how much tracking error to accept would be based on our experience with a large number of investors. The choices of investors *reveal* their tolerances for risk and provide a context for this decision.

Conclusion

This presentation introduces a framework for analyzing risk and return in the presence of taxes to solve two common problems. The first problem has to do with total risk and the diversification of a concentrated holding. The second has to do with tracking error and the diversification of a portfolio.

For a client with a risky stock and a long-term horizon, the recommendation is to diversify most of the concentrated holding. The diversification plan is sensitive to the liquidation horizon, the stock volatility, the cost basis, and any excess return assumptions.

Practitioners need academic help in expanding their thinking about questions of market efficiency in the presence of taxes. I would like to encourage the academic community to further explore such issues. For example, a model like the capital asset pricing model that includes taxes would be a very useful tool.

Figure 8. Trade-Off between Tracking Error and Tax Cost for a Taxable Portfolio

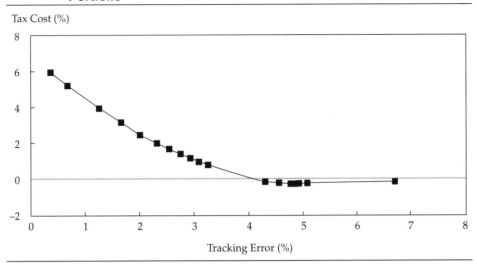

Figure 9. Trade-Off between Excess Return and Tracking Error for Tax-Exempt Portfolio

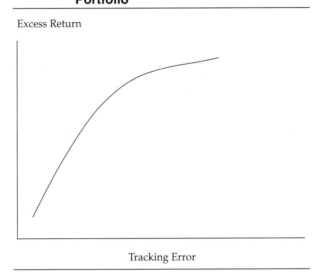

Question and Answer Session

David M. Stein

Question: Are you using this model in portfolios managed by your firm to decide how much of the undiversified assets to sell and how to rebalance?

Stein: We mainly provide diversified equity portfolio management. We are constantly making a trade-off between the tracking-error risk of a portfolio and the tax cost of reducing this risk. With all due respect to Joel Dickson, one of the problems with an index fund is that it must pay a tax cost in order to achieve nearly perfect tracking.[1] A serious portfolio manager must decide whether the improved tracking is worth this cost for each individual investor. If the investor is willing to endure a slight wobble in performance relative to the benchmark, the portfolio manager can improve performance. This is an important consideration in our portfolio management, and we deal with it every day.

Question: Given a 10-year horizon, what would your model recommend for an investor who has a single-security portfolio with low volatility but who wants to buy a high-volatility portfolio?

Stein: In my framework, I would need to know what the investor would get in return for the higher volatility. A specific quantitative assumption about the extra return that the investor expects would enter into the mathematics. The model would identify a curve on which I would be able to choose the decision point. Depending on the expected extra return, the model might either recommend

the high-volatility diversification or suggest that higher volatility is not worth the tax cost. An alternative way of making the investment might be to borrow money and leverage into the market.

Question: How do the results change if the portfolio is not liquidated at the end of the period?

Stein: If you don't plan to liquidate the portfolio at the end of the period, this framework will drive you toward less diversification. Not diversifying may provide a big tax benefit because the investor—or more accurately, the investor's heirs—may get a step-up in cost basis at the end of the period, which is of real economic value.

Question: Given the problems with benchmarks, such as the S&P 500, not being efficient, if you believe in random walk and in positive alpha generation, why should one be concerned with tracking error?

Stein: First, I am not necessarily talking about tracking error to the S&P 500. The S&P 500 is only one particular example of a benchmark. Simply substitute whatever index represents the market you're investing in. As a tax-efficient portfolio manager, I am personally uncomfortable with stepping too far away from market consensus averages, unless I am very confident in my alpha generation. If you believe that markets are not efficient and that you have a positive alpha, by all means, step away from the index and let your investor take the risk. But I would argue that you still need to be extremely concerned about the tax cost of your actions.

Question: Can you explain why it is that the longer the horizon, the more the stock should be diversified?

Stein: The longer the horizon, the uglier the final distribution is. An ugly final distribution has a cost, and the longer the horizon, the greater the cost is. For example, if you're holding a volatile stock, you're not as concerned about what it will do over the course of one day as you are about what it will do over 20 years. For a volatile stock, as time grows, the ugliness gets more extreme. The longer you live with an extremely volatile stock, the more bad things there are that can happen to it.

Question: Given that your approach assumes that mean–variance analysis works, how strongly do you believe in mean–variance analysis?

Stein: My approach does not assume that mean–variance analysis works. Mean–variance analysis provides a framework for thinking about the problem. My work proposes a model for thinking about taxes and diversification and is connected to standard, well-respected concepts in the industry. If you have a utility function that differs or do not want to deal with the Sharpe ratio or the relationship between mean and variance, you need to build a different framework. I would love to see alternatives.

Question: Are you convinced that the Sharpe ratio is the best measure of return efficiency and that beta is the best measure of a stock's relative volatility?

[1] See Mr. Dickson's presentation in this proceedings.

Stein: I'm not convinced that the Sharpe ratio and beta are always the best such measures. The Sharpe ratio is a useful measure because it is easy to think about in the context of this diversification problem. I intend this framework as an *example* of how to choose a decision point. Similarly, beta is not always perfect. In the examples in this presentation, I assume that both the stock and the benchmark have the same beta; if they have different betas, I adjust the mathematics. Again, my presentation offers a framework for thinking about a particular type of problem but does not solve everyone's problems. An academic discussion about Sharpe ratios and beta is beyond my scope.

Question: If an investor came to you with a portfolio composed of a single, volatile, low-cost-basis stock plus cash, would the best course still be to liquidate the risky stock immediately, or is a better approach to use the cash to diversify and then average out of the risky stock while harvesting losses?

Stein: If you have cash, you may not need to diversify quite as much. In effect, having cash is similar to having a stock with a higher cost basis, in which case you also don't need to diversify quite as much. Time is an important aspect of the question. You can diversify today, or you can think about phasing in a diversification program over time. In this presenta-
tion, I have not addressed the issue of timing, a challenge that managers must grapple with continually in the real world. This highlights another big difference between tax-sensitive portfolio management and tax-exempt portfolio management. In taxable portfolio management, timing matters. In tax-exempt portfolio management, the notion of timing is not as critical. A very useful approach is to diversify part of the portfolio to begin the process and, over time, to exploit losses realized in the new portfolio in order to further unwind low-cost-basis initial holdings.

Inflation-Protected Securities in an Asset Allocation Framework

Ivan Rudolph-Shabinsky, CFA
Senior Portfolio Manager, Fixed Income
Sanford C. Bernstein and Company, Inc.

Most investors do not fully appreciate the advantages of U.S. Treasury inflation-protected securities. TIPS offer attractive yields, and their low risk and low correlation with other assets allow investment managers to use them as another tool for optimization within an asset allocation framework. The immaturity of the TIPS market, however, means that investors looking to benefit from these attractive securities might approach them with an element of caution.

U.S. Treasury inflation-protected securities provide two important benefits to investors. First, TIPS offer a yield to maturity of more than 4 percent after inflation—that is, a 4 percent real yield. Second, they are guaranteed by the U.S. government and thus have no credit risk. Furthermore, their high real yields compare favorably with the historical returns of conventional U.S. T-bonds after inflation. Consider the following historical returns: Over the 1926–98 period, intermediate T-bonds had a return of 2.2 percent after inflation. Over the 1960–1998 period, which limits the data to the modern era of fixed income, intermediate T-bonds had a real return of 3.1 percent. As of August 31, 1999, TIPS of 2007 offered a real yield of 4.1 percent.

Simply put, TIPS are an attractive asset class. If investors can earn 4 percent after inflation on a security guaranteed by the U.S. government, they should probably hold some of that security in their portfolios. The question, therefore, is not whether to include TIPS in a portfolio but how much to include in proportion to other asset classes. This presentation examines TIPS by focusing on asset allocation in a real, inflation-adjusted, framework. Most investors ignore inflation and think in terms of a nominal framework. Analyzing asset allocation in real terms allows portfolio managers to make a better match between assets and liabilities.

Nominal Historical Performance

When looking at asset allocation, the first thing to do is to calculate the expected returns for the asset classes under consideration. For example, according to San-

ford C. Bernstein's estimates, the following long-term returns are expected: for T-bills, 4 percent; intermediate T-bonds, 6 percent; and stocks, 9 percent. What is important is not the expected absolute numbers but the relative performance of the asset classes. Bonds should outperform T-bills by 2 percentage points, and stocks should outperform bonds by 3 percentage points. (These estimates are reasonable estimates, but actual performance, of course, may differ.)

Along with expected returns of these three asset classes, investors also need to understand the corresponding risks. For the 1960–98 period, the nominal risk, defined as standard deviation relative to expected return of each asset class, was as follows: T-bills, 0.6 percent; intermediate T-bonds, 8.8 percent; and stocks, 16.2 percent. In choosing an asset class, investors should consider both risk and expected return. T-bills, for example, have the lowest risk but also the lowest expected return of any asset class in this group.

Next, consider the nominal return correlations among these asset classes, as shown in **Table 1**. When stocks have risen, T-bills have usually declined, and vice versa. The correlation between intermediate T-bonds and stocks has been a modestly positive 0.4.

The three sets of assumptions—expected returns, risks, and correlations—can then be put into an optimization model to identify the efficient frontiers for a particular investor's risk aversion. **Figure 1** shows the efficient frontiers for these three asset classes, from a low-risk investor invested almost entirely in T-bills to an average-risk investor with a 60/40 mix of stocks and bonds—a portfolio which would fall on the line

Table 1. Historical Nominal Correlations for T-Bills, T-Bonds, and U.S. Stocks, 1960–98

	T-Bills	T-Bonds	Stocks
T-Bills	1.0		
T-Bonds	−0.4	1.0	
Stocks	−0.2	0.4	1.0

Source: Based on estimated data from Street Software and Sanford C. Bernstein.

right in the middle of this framework—to a risk-loving investor invested entirely in stocks.

How TIPS Affect Asset Allocation

The nominal yield of conventional intermediate T-bonds has two components—real yield and expected inflation—whereas TIPS have only a real yield. Currently, intermediate T-bonds are quoted at a nominal yield of about 6 percent while TIPS offer a real yield of about 4.1 percent. The difference is a measure of investors' inflation expectations and,

according to theory, constitutes a risk premium. In effect, because expectations of inflation may be wrong, investors want to build an insurance premium into the yield of nominal, or noninflation-protected, bonds.

With TIPS, investors receive the real yield *and* the benefit of the U.S. Treasury adjusting the principal of these securities to keep pace with inflation. Consider the example of an investor who bought TIPS with a face value of $100. If inflation for the year ran at 2 percent, the principal of the bonds would increase 2 percent at the end of the year, and the coupons would be calculated on this new principal of $102. Both the coupons and the principal would keep pace with inflation.

To figure TIPS into an asset allocation framework, as described earlier in this presentation, investors should know the expected return. The total return in the long run should be somewhat less than that of conventional intermediate T-bonds, because TIPS are a lower-risk asset and the investor does not need the extra yield of the inflation-risk premium that is built into conventional intermediate T-bonds. Sanford C. Bernstein's estimates show that intermediate

Figure 1. Conventional Asset Allocation in a Nominal Framework for One-Year Horizon

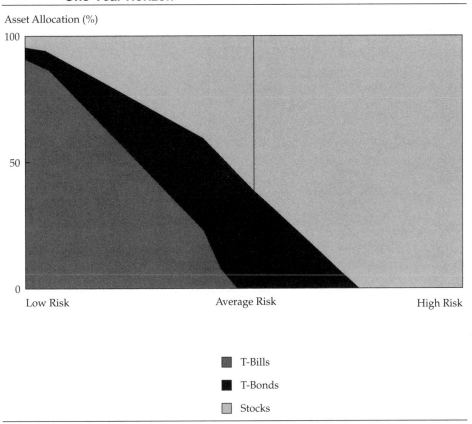

T-bonds have a risk premium of about 50 basis points relative to intermediate TIPS. Thus, when expected returns are evaluated in a long-term framework for an asset allocation study, the expected return for TIPS is 50 bps lower than for conventional bonds.

To determine expected risk for TIPS, consider the volatility of real yields in the United States. TIPS have been very stable, as shown in **Figure 2**. Yields on conventional T-bonds of comparable maturity were considerably more volatile than the yield for TIPS of 2007. Although the more than two years of TIPS history in the United States might convince some investors that TIPS have little risk in terms of their price volatility, such a limited amount of experience is not enough to gauge what might happen in the future. One way to gain perspective, however, is to evaluate inflation-linked bonds in two other countries that have used similar securities for a number of years.

The United Kingdom, which has the longest history with inflation-linked bonds, has used them since the early 1980s. As shown in **Figure 3**, "linkers," as inflation-protected bonds are called in the United Kingdom, have also been more stable in terms of yield than comparable conventional bonds, called "gilts." The linkers' yields have varied between approximately 2 and 4 percent, whereas the long gilts have ranged from a high of 13 percent to a low of about 4 percent.

A similar scenario has played out in the Canadian market, as shown in **Figure 4**. The Canadian long inflation-linked bonds—called real-return bonds, or RRBs—have also had much less volatility in their yields than conventional bonds.

To put TIPS into an asset allocation framework, the estimated risk for TIPS is set lower relative to conventional bonds—7.6 percent for TIPS versus 8.8 percent for intermediate T-bonds. This risk is not much lower than that of conventional bonds for two reasons. First, because of their low coupons, TIPS have very long durations, so even a small change in real yields will have a fairly significant impact on their prices. Second, setting the risk at 7.6 percent errs on the conservative side because although real yields have not moved much recently (particularly in the United States), they can still move more in the future.

Some of the most interesting aspects of TIPS are seen within the correlations between TIPS returns and those for T-bills, intermediate T-bonds, and stocks. Sanford C. Bernstein's estimates in **Table 2** show that TIPS have low correlations with the other asset classes: 0.2 with T-bills, 0.3 with bonds, and 0.0

Figure 2. Real Yields for TIPS and Comparable T-Bonds, January 30, 1997, through August 31, 1999

Source: Based on data from Bankers Trust.

Figure 3. Yields for U.K. Conventional Government Bonds and Inflation-Protected Bonds, 1982–99

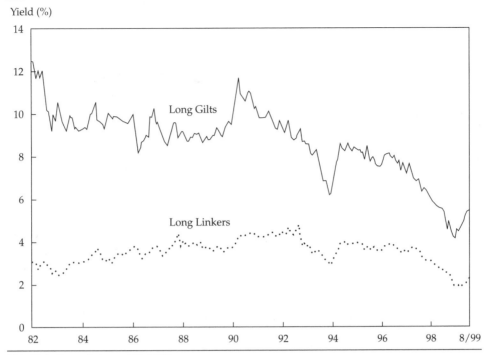

Note: Data through August 31, 1999.

Source: Based on data from Bankers Trust.

Figure 4. Yields for Canadian Conventional Government Bonds and Inflation-Protected Bonds, 1992–99

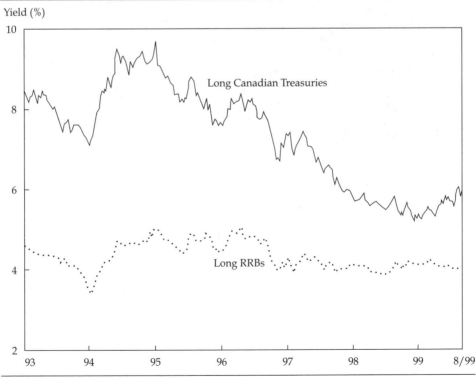

Note: Data through August 31, 1999.

Table 2. Historical Nominal Correlations for T-Bills, TIPS, T-Bonds, and U.S. Stocks 1960–98[a]

	T-Bills	TIPS	T-Bonds	Stocks
T-Bills	1.0			
TIPS	0.2	1.0		
T-Bonds	–0.4	0.3	1.0	
Stocks	–0.2	0.0	0.4	1.0

Note: Data for 1960–98 period from the United Kingdom, Canada, and the United States used to make assumptions about future TIPS performance.

[a] TIPS data simulated for 1960–98 period.

Source: Based on estimated data from Street Software and Sanford C. Bernstein.

with stocks. These low correlations are what make TIPS so attractive in the asset allocation framework.

Based on the risk and return data for T-bills, intermediate T-bonds, and stocks and given a one-year investment horizon, TIPS squeeze out bonds considerably when an optimizer is used to create efficient portfolios. As **Figure 5** shows, the average investor would have almost no conventional intermediate T-bonds and would have a portfolio mostly made up of stocks and TIPS. Note that the low-risk investor would still be invested primarily in T-bills.

TIPS in a Real Framework

When considered after the impact of inflation, the riskiness of TIPS declines, as shown in **Table 3**. With this lowered risk, TIPS take an even larger role in the asset allocation framework, as shown in **Figure 6**. Even in the portfolio with the lowest risk, TIPS squeeze out T-bills for part of the portfolio, and conventional intermediate T-bonds play almost no role in an efficient portfolio.

Return, of course, is not independent of risk, and the assumptions used for setting a one-year framework are not appropriate for a horizon of 5, 10, 15, or 20 years. **Table 4** shows different risk expectations for different time horizons. A five-year period is more appropriate for evaluating risk than a one-year period;

Figure 5. Effect of TIPS on Asset Allocation in a Nominal Framework with One-Year Horizon

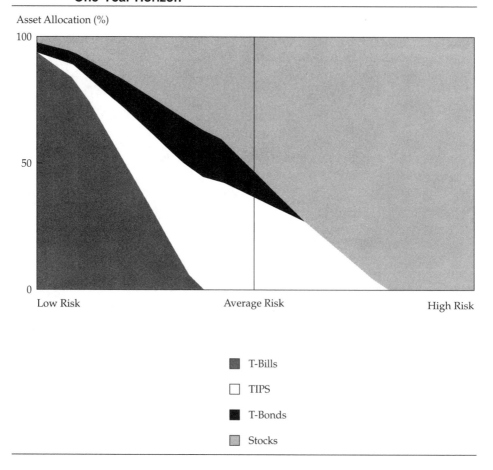

- ■ T-Bills
- □ TIPS
- ■ T-Bonds
- ▨ Stocks

Table 3. Real and Nominal Risk, 1960–98[a]

Asset	Nominal Risk	Real Risk
T-bills	0.6%	1.8%
TIPS	7.6	6.3
T-bonds	8.8	8.2
Stocks	16.2	16.4

Note: Data from the United Kingdom, Canada, and the United States used to make assumptions about future TIPS performance.

[a]TIPS data simulated for 1960–98 period.

Source: Based on estimated data from Street Software and Sanford C. Bernstein.

Table 4. Effect of Horizon on Expected Real Risk

Asset	One-Year Horizon	Five-Year Horizon
T-bills	1.8%	3.8%
TIPS	6.3	5.5
T-bonds	8.2	9.2
Stocks	16.4	14.9

Note: Risk expectations based on 1960–98 data.

it is more consistent with what investors want and investors can identify how the risk changes as the horizon is extended. With a five-year horizon in a real framework, the risk of TIPS falls even lower—from 6.3 percent to 5.5 percent.

Two differences from the one-year horizon are of note. First, the risk of T-bills rises. The return on

T-bills is primarily a function of short-term interest rates and inflation, which are two variables that can be predicted with confidence for only a short-term horizon. Over a five-year horizon, investing in T-bills becomes much riskier. Second, the risk on stocks actually drops over long horizons.

In a five-year framework, TIPS take on an even more dominant role. As **Figure 7** shows, TIPS represent almost half of the low-risk portfolio and the rest of the portfolios are primarily a combination of stocks and TIPS.

Figure 6. Effect of TIPS on Asset Allocation in a Real Framework with One-Year Horizon

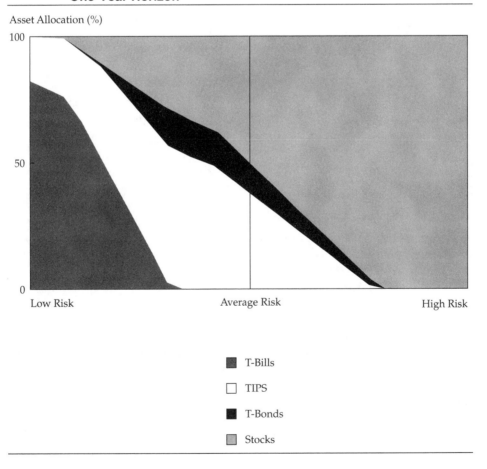

Figure 7. Effect of TIPS on Asset Allocation in a Real Framework with a Five-Year Horizon

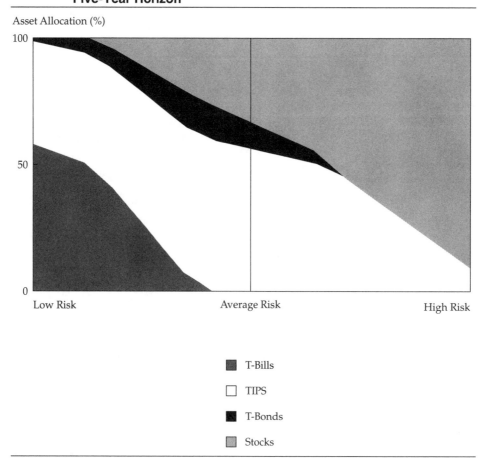

Practical Considerations

Although TIPS are certainly attractive, some caveats must be noted. First, the methodology used in this presentation has limitations. Second, for the purpose of simplification, some of the practical considerations of investing in TIPS have not been covered.

Methodology. All of the assumptions in this presentation are conservative and are based on the long term. For example, even though the expected return for TIPS is assumed to be 50 bps lower than for intermediate T-bonds, TIPS still play a large role in an optimal portfolio.

Also, the data used in this study were true as of August 31, 1999 (and remained true on November 9, 1999), with real yields at slightly more than 4 percent. Conventional Treasury yields on off-the-run Treasuries (not on-the-run Treasuries, which have slightly lower yields) are about 6.1 percent for similar maturities, as shown in **Figure 8**. If the real yield of a little more than 4 percent is added to expected inflation as measured by economists' consensus inflation forecasts (about 2.4 percent over the next 10

years), TIPS will offer a return that exceeds intermediate T-bonds by about 35 bps. Clearly, if such an expected return was used in this presentation, intermediate T-bonds would play no role at all and TIPS would be much more attractive.

Another caveat is that, although intermediate T-bonds are the only alternative to TIPS considered in this presentation, other options exist. For example, mortgage-backed securities and corporate bonds certainly offer much higher yields than intermediate T-bonds. Adding 75 bps of return for mortgage-backed securities or corporate bonds makes bonds more compelling. As shown in **Figure 9**, the 60/40 investor in a nominal framework would still have a 60/40 mix in the real framework, but the mix would be 60 percent stocks, 20 percent bonds, and 20 percent TIPS, which is the theoretically optimal portfolio for most investors before taxes.

Some municipal inflation-protected securities (MIPS) are also available, and at Sanford C. Bernstein, we have used them in our taxable accounts. Although the MIPS market is even more thinly traded than the TIPS market, some municipalities are willing to issue

Figure 8. TIPS Pricing, as of August 31, 1999

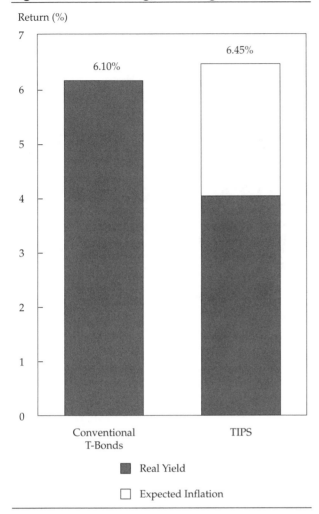

Deflation is another potential problem not accounted for in this presentation. If TIPS experience deflation, the Treasury guarantees that, at maturity, investors will always get back $100 of principal. So, if deflation occurred over the next 10 years, investors who bought TIPS today would still get back $100 of principal. Such protection may not be worth much, because in the interim, investors would see a drop in their principal and a reduction in their coupons. Only the final payment would guarantee that they would get $100 back. The likelihood of long-term deflation, however, is very small and thus the risk is given little weight.

Investing in TIPS. Investors interested in inflation-linked bonds need to consider more than the theoretically optimal asset allocation. Fundamental practical considerations include the immaturity of the TIPS market, the value of non-U.S. inflation-linked securities for U.S. investors, and investment strategy.

The inflation-protected securities market in the United States is still immature. Only six issues of TIPS are outstanding, and few are being issued, as shown in **Table 5**. The U.S. Treasury issues less than $7 billion of TIPS each quarter, alternating between issuing a 10-year security and a 30-year security. (Note that the mix and frequency of issuance has recently changed). The Treasury issued a 5-year security in the past but has stopped doing so.

inflation-protected securities, and if the demand builds, the supply will appear. Furthermore, investors can synthetically create MIPS in the form of a trust. One method is to buy TIPS and municipal bonds into the trust and short T-bonds; the end result would have the inflation protection of the TIPS in addition to the municipal bond return. Of course, investors would have to consider the tax treatment for such a portfolio.

Indeed, the impact of taxes is an important point to consider and has not been addressed in this presentation. For example, the principal adjustment based on inflation is treated as taxable income. If an investor started off with $100 of principal and had $102 in principal at the end of the year, the uplift from the $2 of inflation would be taxed. The treatment is different in the United Kingdom, where the inflation uplift is not taxed as aggressively. The problem with current U.S. taxation is that if surprisingly high inflation occurred, investors would enjoy some inflation protection but it would be taxed. In such a scenario, investors would not get full inflation protection.

Table 5. Size of TIPS Market, as of October 1999

Coupon	Maturity	Yield	Market Value (billions)
3.625%	2002	3.9%	$17.6
3.375	2007	4.1	16.0
3.625	2008	4.1	17.0
3.875	2009	4.1	16.1
3.625	2028	4.1	15.9
3.875	2029	4.1	14.4
Total TIPS outstanding	—	—	$97.0

Source: Based on data from Barclays Capital.

Compared with other sectors, TIPS represent a fairly small percentage of the fixed-income market, as shown in **Table 6.** The commercial mortgage-backed securities market is considered to be fairly small within the general fixed-income market, but TIPS account for a much smaller proportion of the market in terms of both net issuance and total market value. In short, if every investor in the country wanted to buy TIPS for their portfolios, the market would have a problem.

Figure 9. Asset Allocation in a Real Framework Using Active Management of Bonds with a Five-Year Horizon

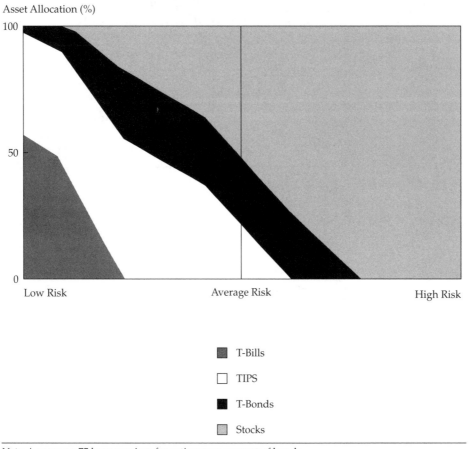

Note: Assumes a 75 bps premium for active management of bonds.

Table 6. Composition of U.S. Fixed-Income Market, as of December 31, 1998

Issuers	1998 Net Issuance (billions)	Outstanding (billions)
Agencies	$279	$1,274
Mortgage pools	182	1,970
Corporates (domestic)		
Investment grade	119	1,878
High yield	113	580
CMBS	83	250
TIPS	28	89

Note: TIPS data as of October 1999.

Non-U.S. markets also offer some opportunities for investing in inflation-linked securities. The inflation that these securities protect against, however, is not U.S. inflation but the inflation in the respective countries. (Inflation protection is also specialized for U.S. TIPS. Because the calculation of TIPS is linked to the nonseasonally adjusted U.S. Consumer Price Index, TIPS offer protection against inflation only as measured by the CPI.) Furthermore, only the United Kingdom has a substantial amount of inflation-linked bonds outstanding, as shown in **Table 7**.

Investors have two choices in terms of the practical use of inflation-linked securities. First, they can use these securities as a separate asset class, perhaps hiring a manager who specializes in inflation-linked bonds. This approach clearly creates a low-risk,

Table 7. Non-U.S. Inflation-Protected Securities Market, as of 1998

Issuers	Expected Total 1999 Issuance (billions)	Outstanding (billions)
United Kingdom	$6	$109
France	6	7
Canada	1	8
Sweden	0	13
Australia	1	4

diversifying component in the overall asset allocation. In such a case, guidelines sometimes allow the
use of non-U.S. inflation-linked bonds or even bonds
that are not inflation linked at all. The overall low-
risk, diversifying mandate, however, should be the
highest priority. Another approach is to make TIPS
part of a benchmark for an existing fixed-income
manager. For instance, a benchmark could consist of
80 percent Lehman Brothers Aggregate Index and 20
percent TIPS, which would encourage the manager
to maintain about 20 percent of the portfolio in
inflation-linked bonds over time. This strategy
offers potential added value if the manager is able
to move tactically and profitably between inflation-
linked bonds and conventional bonds.

Conclusion

Relatively new and thinly traded, TIPS are currently
an underappreciated asset class that deserves careful
consideration for inclusion in portfolios with a variety
of risk profiles. TIPS offer investors attractive real
yields, inflation protection, and government guarantees. When used in an optimized asset allocation
framework, TIPS improve the overall risk–return profile available to investors. The theoretical framework
provided suggests that a typical investor's optimal
asset mix is 60/20/20 (stocks, bonds, and TIPS), but
practical considerations, mainly the relatively small
size of this asset class, might point to a slightly smaller
TIPS allocation.

Question and Answer Session

Ivan Rudolph-Shabinsky, CFA

Question: In the example of Figure 8, are bond investors expecting an inflation rate of 2.0–2.05 percent, not 2.4–2.5 percent?

Rudolph-Shabinsky: An expected inflation rate of 2.0–2.05 percent is one explanation. Another explanation is that these securities are new and actually represent a risk to current investors, many of whom are buying TIPS as an opportunistic investment rather than with a view to using them as a new asset class. Some investment managers realize that TIPS are attractively priced and are using them opportunistically relative to conventional bonds. With this approach, TIPS become a little bit riskier because they introduce tracking error. They are not in the benchmark, so investors require a premium to own these securities. If the majority of investors are active bond managers who view TIPS as risky, the fact that TIPS would offer higher expected returns than intermediate T-bonds is not surprising. This situation should change as more strategic investors move into this market.

Question: If the CPI is a fraud, as some contend, and it is adjusted or some other inflation index is used, what are the implications for TIPS?

Rudolph-Shabinsky: TIPS are adjusted according to the CPI. The Treasury has said that if the CPI were to be fundamentally changed or replaced, it would maintain a series similar to the existing CPI calculation with which to adjust outstanding TIPS. Smaller, more-incremental changes are risks specific to TIPS that the investor undertakes.

Question: How is duration calculated for TIPS? For example, what would be the approximate duration for the 2002 or 2007 TIPS?

Rudolph-Shabinsky: The answer is complicated. As with any other bond, if duration is thought of as the price sensitivity of a bond to changes in its own yield, then duration is easy to calculate. If duration is thought of as the price sensitivity to nominal yields, it is difficult to calculate.

The relationship between real yield and nominal yield is not easy to understand. Nominal yield has three components: real yield, expected inflation, and the inflation risk-premium. If nominal yield rises by 1 percent, which of the three components caused it to rise? Unless you can predict the relationship between real yields and nominal yields, calculating the nominal duration of TIPS is difficult. The empirically measured nominal duration in the United States has actually been close to zero, as most moves in nominal yields have taken place with few, if any, changes in TIPS yields.

The relationship between the mathematical duration of TIPS and their estimated nominal duration changes as maturity changes. As a bond shortens, the relationship between real and nominal yield becomes much tighter, so its mathematical duration and its nominal duration come closer and closer together. In other words, for the 2002 TIPS, you might believe that the nominal duration is 0.4 times its mathematical duration of about two and a half years, whereas for the 2007 TIPS, the number might be 0.3 times the mathematical duration of about seven years. For the longest bonds—the 30-year

variety—the number might be 0.2 times the mathematical duration of about 17 years. For a more detailed explanation, see my article with Frank Trainer in the *Financial Analysts Journal*.[1]

Question: What adjustments did you consider in analyzing the data on Canadian and U.K. inflation-protected securities?

Rudolph-Shabinsky: In the United Kingdom, for example, Sanford C. Bernstein looked at the interrelationships between inflation-linked gilts, conventional gilts, and the U.K. stock market and then made adjustments based on whether similar relationships would exist in the United States. Obviously, some differences exist between U.S. and non-U.S. markets. For example, the United Kingdom not only has had a different economic history in terms of inflation, but because of some tax implications, U.K. inflation-linked bonds trade differently from U.S. TIPS.

Question: Given that some observers have suggested that the standard deviation of TIPS resembles that of a one-year Treasury issue, why are your estimated standard deviations much higher than for one-year Treasury issues?

Rudolph-Shabinsky: At Sanford C. Bernstein, we wanted to be conservative. If you put TIPS into the asset allocation calculation at even lower risk, they would take up more of the portfolio. Also, the

---

[1] Ivan Rudolph-Shabinsky and Francis H. Trainer, Jr., "Assigning a Duration to Inflation-Protected Bonds," *Financial Analysts Journal* (September/October 1999):53–59.

risk is that real yields may change. Nothing states that real yields can't move up, and given that the TIPS of 2002 have a two-and-a-half-year duration in terms of real yields, if real yields moved up to 100 bps, the price on those TIPS would change by 2.5 times. The 30-year TIPS, which are the longest ones available, have mathematical durations of about 17 or 18 years, so if you had a 1 percent change in real yields, you would be looking at a very large change in price. Although 30-year TIPS haven't changed much in price, they could, which is a potential that has been incorporated into the data used in this presentation.

Question: What causes changes in real yields?

Rudolph-Shabinsky: Changes in real yields involve many factors. In the long run, changes occur because of underlying economic growth and productivity in the economy. Many people think changes in the short run are related to changes in the Federal Reserve's fund rate, which has an impact on short-term real yields that carries through for longer maturities. What has been true in the United States is that when the Fed has increased the short rate, real rates, as measured by TIPS yields, have generally increased because of the concern that real rates are rising.

Question: If bonds have fallen recently because of inflation concerns, why have TIPS yields gone up?

Rudolph-Shabinsky: TIPS yields have risen, but not as much as Treasury yields, so TIPS have outperformed Treasuries. When inflation expectations are rising, the nominal yield starts to rise and the price of nominal bonds falls. If the relationship between nominal and real yields was fully a function of changes in expected inflation, a rise in interest rates would have no impact on the price of TIPS because the real yield wouldn't change. Nevertheless, a relationship seems to exist between nominal and real yields; when nominal yields rose approximately 1 percent in 1999, the rise was caused mostly by changes in inflation expectations but also by an increase in real yield. Perhaps the market believed that if inflation seemed likely to pick up, the Fed was going to have to raise rates and, therefore, the real yield would have gone up somewhat as well. TIPS have outperformed nominal bonds this year because TIPS yields have risen considerably less than nominal yields.

Question: Is a liquidity premium currently built into TIPS pricing?

Rudolph-Shabinsky: Yes, but figuring out what part is a liquidity premium and what part is a novelty premium is difficult. Their liquidity is fairly good. This market is thinly traded, but TIPS are more liquid than most corporate bonds. They're simply less liquid than the most liquid T-bonds.

Question: What is the smallest portfolio size that would make sense for active management of a TIPS portfolio?

Rudolph-Shabinsky: From a business perspective, Sanford C. Bernstein won't manage portfolios of less than $3 million. But you could probably manage a smaller portfolio; you can get odd-lot execution on TIPS without paying too much of a price penalty.

Question: Does purchasing specific issues of TIPS make sense for a buy-and-hold strategy?

Rudolph-Shabinsky: A buy-and-hold strategy with TIPS suffers from the same problems that conventional bonds have. If you chose a buy-and-hold strategy, the biggest concern would be making sure that you're matching your liabilities. You would get the same inflation uplift whether you bought a 2-year, 5-year, 10-year, or a 30-year bond. Thus, you could maintain your inflation protection by holding long TIPS or simply rolling over shorter-maturity TIPS. To lock in today's real yields, however, requires matching the real duration of your TIPS holdings to the duration of your liabilities.

Question: Do managers have an opportunity to deliver significant incremental alpha if a portfolio is managed using the available non-U.S. inflation-linked bonds, and what would be the inherent risks of such a strategy?

Rudolph-Shabinsky: Using non-U.S. inflation-linked bonds would probably add a limited amount of alpha, unless aggressive strategies were used. In our view, this asset class is attractive because it is low risk. Taking on aggressive active-management strategies, therefore, makes little sense. The primary risk would be change in foreign exchange rates, but of course, this risk could be hedged. The more important risk over time is that non-U.S. inflation-linked bonds don't protect against U.S. inflation.

Question: Given that your model contains assumptions about the risk–return trade-off and correlations, how sensitive are the assumptions and are some assumptions more critical than others?

Rudolph-Shabinsky: Correlations are the most sensitive area, which makes the stress-testing of correlations critical. If correlations turned out to be very different than what they've been historically, the scenario would change. For example, if TIPS became very highly correlated with bonds or stocks, the biggest concern would be that they wouldn't provide diversification benefits. After considering inflation-protected securities in three different countries for significant periods of time and evaluating the data from a theoretical perspective, at Sanford C. Bernstein, we believe that low correlation is likely to be maintained.

Question: TIPS are often suggested as an inflation hedge in which investor's liabilities are inflation linked, but doesn't the low inflation duration of TIPS suggest that the hedge provided by them does not extend beyond the dollars actually invested in them?

Rudolph-Shabinsky: Yes, the protection from TIPS applies only to the amount of money invested, unless leverage is used. The other risk people should be aware of is the linkage to the CPI as measured by the Bureau of Labor Statistics, because the inflation to which investors' liabilities are subject may differ from the CPI.

Question: How do TIPS perform in bull or bear markets or in strong or weak economies, and

what are the implications for their use in the U.S. economy?

Rudolph-Shabinsky: In the United States, TIPS underperformed conventional bonds dramatically in 1997 and 1998. As inflation expectations continued to fall, TIPS did very poorly relative to conventional bonds. TIPS performance stopped declining when the breakeven inflation rate between TIPS and conventional bonds (the difference in their yields) was down to about 65–75 bps. Since then, their breakeven inflation rate has been rising and is now at about 2 percent and TIPS have been outperforming relative to conventional intermediate T-bonds and most other conventional types of bonds. TIPS outperform when inflation expectations are rising and underperform when inflation expectations are falling. Inflation can rise in a variety of economic circumstances, but you would expect inflation to rise when the economy is growing strongly, as it has recently in the United States. As the U.S. economy has recently shown, however, strong economic growth does not always lead to rising inflation.

Question: How do you determine fair value for TIPS?

Rudolph-Shabinsky: In the long-term relationship, an inflation-risk premium is built into conventional bonds. If the real yield plus likely inflation was compared with nominal bonds and the result was an expected total yield higher than for conventional bonds, TIPS would be inexpensive and should be purchased tactically. On the other hand, if the inflation-risk premium was to become very high, which would happen if people got worried about inflation, people would build more of an inflation-risk premium into the nominal bond and TIPS would not be as attractive. Such considerations form our main valuation criteria.

Question: Over the long term, will the advantage of TIPS be muted because the interest on short-maturity bonds will provide some inflation protection in and of itself?

Rudolph-Shabinsky: Consider T-bills, for example. They keep up with inflation but don't offer much of a real yield. As inflation expectations rise, interest rates rise, and investors can reinvest at higher rates. But our asset allocation study shows that TIPS are more attractive.

Tax-Efficient Mutual Funds

Joel M. Dickson
Principal
The Vanguard Group, Inc.

Conventional wisdom says that most mutual funds are tax inefficient and that mutual fund investors who seek to limit taxes should stick with index funds. If managed appropriately, however, mutual funds can be tax efficient, even for high-net-worth investors.

According to reports in the financial press, many investors are spurning mutual funds because they want more control over their personal tax situations. Indeed, mutual funds have not proven to be tax efficient, but the tax argument against mutual funds is a bit overblown. This presentation argues that mutual funds can be constructed to be not only tax efficient but also more tax efficient than separate accounts in certain instances. Individual investors may have more control over separately managed accounts, but other issues should be considered in regard to the tax efficiency of mutual funds.

Mutual Funds and Tax Efficiency

On average, mutual funds have not been tax efficient. Over the past five years, an investor in the highest marginal federal tax bracket could expect a disappointing average after-tax return, as shown in **Table 1** for various categories of equity mutual funds. For example, the average mutual fund in the large-capitalization category had an average after-tax return of 17.2 percent in annualized return and the pretax return was higher by 2.6 percentage points a year. For the high-income taxable investor, taxes have been the single greatest cost of mutual fund management, eating up an average of 2.5 percentage points each year over the past five years, with a similar number for the past 10 years. Furthermore, 2.5 percentage points is greater than both the average expense ratios among funds and the estimated transaction costs associated with portfolio turnover among funds.

Similarly, other segments of the mutual fund market—whether mid-cap or small-cap stocks or balanced funds—do not provide much relief. Balanced funds hold taxable bonds as a portion of the portfolio, so on a relative basis, they are hit even harder. Small-

cap stocks take less of a tax bite in absolute percentage terms, although as a percentage of return, they take a little bit more than large-cap stocks. In fact, taxes are often worse for small-cap funds because successful stocks tend to grow out of their universe, which forces portfolio managers to sell them and realize the capital gain. Small-cap funds, however, may also represent an opportunity from a tax-management perspective because there are more potential taxes to eliminate. In short, although the story about mutual funds, on average, is not good, the phrase "on average" is significant; it means that tax-efficient mutual funds can exist or be structured.

Some types of funds are more tax efficient than others. Index funds have better tax efficiency than other funds, particularly large-cap and total-market index funds. Large-cap index funds such as those based on the S&P 500 Index or the Wilshire 5000 Index have certainly been tax efficient. Surprisingly, reports in the financial press suggest that *all* index funds are more tax efficient than other mutual funds, but such is not the case for small-cap index funds, in which successful stocks tend to grow out of the index. The Russell 2000 Index, for example, reconstitutes itself every June 30 and thus causes sudden turnover on one day each year.

Although nothing makes an actively managed, tax-efficient mutual fund impossible, combining the terms "actively managed" and "tax efficient" seems to be an oxymoron among mutual fund managers. The real cause of mutual funds' tax inefficiency is that gains are not realized at the discretion of the investor. The portfolio manager has the capability to affect an individual's tax bill and thus may create an unwanted tax liability, and investors lose some timing ability when they give a portfolio manager authority over

Table 1. Mutual Fund Tax Efficiency for Five Years Ending December 31, 1998

Type of Fund	Average Annual Return	
	After-Tax Return	Lost to Taxes
Large-cap	17.2%	2.6%
Mid-cap	12.8	2.7
Small-cap	9.0	2.2
Balanced	10.4	2.9

Note: Calculations assume account is not liquidated at the end of the period.

Source: Based on Morningstar data.

their tax bill. Investors with low income might want to realize more gains; investors with high income usually do not want to realize gains. Regardless of income level, investors might prefer to take gains when they have losses to offset them. Whether the result of an investment in a mutual fund or a separate account, taxes are a cost that can be controlled to a certain extent because the tax code is known and taxable events can be managed.

The central focus of this presentation is equity mutual funds. In the mutual fund world, fixed-income investors have a choice between taxable bonds and municipal bonds, and they can choose the best vehicle for their own tax situation. On the equity side, investors generally do not have such discretion. The equity mutual fund universe has not divided into different tax clienteles, as happened on the fixed-income side through the advent of the municipal bond fund, but the marketplace is driving equity mutual funds toward greater segmentation. Of course, investing in equities offers the most control over tax realizations because capital gains remain untaxed until realized. As James Poterba notes, unrealized gains represent a contingent future tax liability, but by not realizing gains, investors incur no *current* tax liability and retain more control over their individual future tax situation.[1] For example, investors can use appreciated stocks for charitable deductions or pass the stocks through their estates. Also, a big discrepancy exists between short-term and long-term capital gains tax rates, and investors in a high-income tax bracket face, in effect, a double tax burden for short-term gains and dividends.

Evaluating Tax Efficiency

Most people think that evaluating a mutual fund's tax efficiency is simply a matter of looking at turnover. The subject, however, is considerably more complex. Covering the intricacies of the tax code alone would require a serious commitment of time. Despite such complexity, the main considerations fall into two basic categories: evaluating the funds themselves and evaluating portfolio managers.

Evaluating Funds. Investment managers who work with individual investors must consider a myriad of factors when evaluating the tax efficiency of mutual funds, including investment strategy, the character of portfolio holdings, turnover strategy, accounting procedures, and shareholder activity, just to name a few.

■ *Investment strategy.* A mutual fund's investment strategy—whether growth, value, or small-cap or large-cap stocks—may affect its overall tax efficiency. All else equal, large-cap equity funds tend to have better tax efficiency than most other types of funds. Small-cap stocks suffer from the problem of growing out of their universe. For example, consistent small-cap managers who started holding Intel when it went public nearly three decades ago may have had to scale back the position because it grew too large in proportion to the rest of the portfolio, and eventually, they had to sell all of their Intel stock because it grew out of the small-cap universe. Furthermore, merger and acquisition (M&A) activity is much more common in the small-cap universe. In the process of dealing with such stocks, small-cap managers tend to realize a lot of gains, so small-cap mutual funds can cause greater tax liability. Nevertheless, the small-cap universe provides potentially greater opportunity to add value on a tax-managed basis.

In general, value stocks, because of their inherently high dividend yields, provide a lower after-tax return. If a value stock becomes a growth stock, as happened with IBM after it fell from grace in the 1980s and then came back, value managers who want to maintain style purity may decide not to hold it. Consequently, value managers may end up selling their best stocks, which have probably grown in the portfolio, and thus may realize a lot of gains.

Growth managers, on the other hand, invest in a relatively tax-efficient universe. In addition to generally lower dividend yields, style constraints do not force these managers to sell a successful growth stock (although other considerations may lead them to sell).

Given such style tendencies, investors need to think about which type of mutual funds they want to hold in taxable accounts. The decision of where to hold a tax-managed value-stock portfolio should be based on the investors' assumption that a fund's pre-tax alpha will be high enough to offset the tax liability. In other words, the focus should be on maximizing the investors' after-tax returns, not minimizing taxes. For example, if an investor thinks value stocks will outperform growth stocks over the long run by more

---

[1]See Mr. Poterba's presentation in this proceedings.

than the difference in tax bite, then value stocks make perfect sense in the taxable account. If, however, the investor thinks pretax returns on value stocks and growth stocks will be similar, then it probably makes sense to hold the value fund in a tax-deferred account.

■ *Character of portfolio holdings.* The character of individual portfolio holdings can also affect tax efficiency. For example, a more tax-efficient fund will stress lower-dividend-yield stocks within the targeted universe. Also, strategies to minimize taxes, such as going short against the box (which has become a lot tougher because of recent changes in tax laws) and protective puts, can be used to improve tax efficiency.

■ *Turnover strategy.* Most people focus on turnover when evaluating tax efficiency because they think that high turnover means less tax efficiency. This belief, however, is not necessarily true. High turnover can mean better tax efficiency for investors who are realizing losses. Consider two index funds that track the S&P 500: One is managed for tax efficiency and one is not. The only difference is that the tax-managed fund harvests losses in order to generate capital losses to offset gains in the portfolio. The regular index fund has a certain level of turnover that is influenced mostly by additions and deletions to the index. The tax-managed fund has the same turnover as the regular fund *plus* the turnover associated with selling losers to offset realized gains. Although the tax-managed fund has higher turnover, it also has greater expected tax efficiency. At best, turnover is an imperfect indicator of tax efficiency.

■ *Accounting procedures.* Accounting procedures, such as decisions on whether to sell high- or low-cost-basis shares, can be powerful tools for minimizing tax burdens in general. Accounting procedures are especially powerful for mutual fund investors because they do not change the pretax return of the portfolio but improve the after-tax return. So, using accounting procedures benefits some of a fund's shareholders, without harming any current shareholders.

■ *Shareholder activity.* A common complaint about mutual funds is that they are subject to cash flows that could affect the tax realizations of the fund. Shareholder redemptions can cause the sales of securities that would, in turn, cause realized gains to be distributed to the shareholders who remain in the fund and do not want that tax liability. Although this phenomenon is a theoretical possibility, simple tax-management techniques can mitigate its likelihood, as discussed below.

Evaluating Manager Performance. In trying to evaluate a mutual fund's tax efficiency, considering the portfolio manager's performance is crucial. Investors should ask four questions about portfolio managers:

■ *How is performance measured?* The key to answering this question is understanding the environment in which managers compete. The mutual fund life cycle has come full circle. During the infancy of mutual funds, from the 1930s through the 1950s, all investors were taxable clients, but in the 1970s and 1980s, with the advent of the IRA and the 401(k), many investors stopped caring about current taxes. Because portfolio managers are most often evaluated based on *pretax* return, they have little or no incentive to manage for *after-tax* return. Furthermore, most managers are compensated relative to a benchmark, and most of the benchmarks are measured on a pretax basis.

■ *Are tax considerations mentioned in the prospectus?* Although tax efficiency is often a fleeting consideration in prospectuses and may not be mentioned at all, a mutual fund's prospectus provides important clues about the fund's tax efficiency. That is, if a manager is taking taxes into account in the day-to-day management of a fund, then it will probably be detailed in the fund's prospectus. My rule of thumb is that if no mention is made of tax-efficient practices in the prospectus, then one must assume that tax efficiency is not being considered in the management of the portfolio.

Historical performance is not a reliable guide because mutual funds change over time. Past tax efficiency does not guarantee future tax efficiency, just as high pretax returns in the past do not guarantee high returns in the future. The prospectus has to be the guiding document as to whether the portfolio is being managed on a pretax or an after-tax basis.

■ *Are all investors' tax goals aligned?* With mutual funds, the major problem for tax efficiency is that they are commingled vehicles and investors' tax concerns often are not aligned. That is, a fund may have pretax investors and after-tax investors, taxable corporate investors and taxable individual investors, and investors with different tax brackets. In such cases, the portfolio manager may be serving many masters.

■ *Does the manager report after-tax returns?* Tax efficiency is the goal of maximizing after-tax return, not necessarily minimizing taxes, which is a significant distinction. Many people tend to confuse after-tax return maximization with tax minimization. The classic and easy case is, of course, municipal bonds versus government bonds. People in the 36 percent tax bracket obviously need to buy municipal bonds, but people in the 28 percent tax bracket can probably get a higher after-tax return from government bonds, even though they end up paying more taxes. Similarly, in the management of an equity portfolio, when managers consider selling a stock because they do not like its prospects, they should decide whether the expected return of the replacement stock is high enough to offset the tax costs of selling the old stock. Although selling the old stock will generate taxable capital gains, if the expected return of the new stock is high enough, the after-tax return will prove superior to holding the old stock.

Tax-Managed Investing

No matter what their investment strategy or shareholder profile, mutual funds can be managed on an after-tax return basis using strategies that fall into four general categories: tax-efficient accounting, trading strategies, portfolio construction, and cash flow stability.

Tax-Efficient Accounting. Discussion about tax-efficient accounting techniques usually centers on HIFO (highest in, first out) accounting. With HIFO accounting, a portfolio manager who decides to sell a security will sell the shares with the highest cost basis first, thereby minimizing the tax burden. Such an approach is not necessarily the most tax efficient, however, because the overall position of the portfolio should be considered. Different methods may work better in different situations. For example, the manager of a gold portfolio or an emerging market portfolio during the past decade might want to realize the lowest cost lots first to use the capital loss carryforwards generated in the portfolio.

Tax-efficient accounting not only is effective but, unlike trading strategies, also does not require a trade-off with pretax return. Consider a portfolio manager who buys 100 shares of XYZ company at $100 a share and later buys 100 shares at $150. The manager decides to sell 100 shares of XYZ stock at $125. With HIFO accounting, the sale realizes a $2,500 loss on the position. With FIFO (first in, first out) accounting, the sale realizes a $2,500 *gain*. Although the pretax return does not change, the after-tax results change as a function of the different accounting techniques.

Tax-efficient accounting is more general than HIFO. Consider the distinction between long-term gains and short-term gains. A portfolio manager might want to realize a higher dollar amount of long-term gains, even though HIFO accounting would lead the manager to realize short-term gains, because the tax burden of the long-term gains might be lower.

Tax-sensitive accounting is most powerful in portfolios that have so-called "position breadth" (that is, the fund bought a lot of a stock over a long period of time and has a greater dispersion of cost lots). In these cases, managers can choose among a wide range of cost lots, with a greater effect on after-tax returns. The positive cash flow of mutual funds, which may not exist in a separate account, increases the effectiveness of accounting techniques because of greater position depth (i.e., more cost lots per position), which often leads to greater position breadth (i.e., dispersion in lot prices) in the portfolio.

Index funds tend not to make concentrated purchases or sales of any particular stock but instead buy small slices of all stocks in the index. Funds experiencing cash inflows will buy small amounts of many stocks with different cost lots every day, so they have many different cost lots and significant position breadth. As an illustration, equity index funds at a large mutual fund complex averaged about 92 different tax lots per security and had a position breadth of about 20 percent, as shown in **Table 2**. Actively managed equity funds have more-concentrated buying and selling. Active managers buy stocks they like today. They tend to buy into positions over a relatively short period of time and also to sell out of them in a short period of time. Thus, actively managed funds tend to have fewer cost lots per security, less position breadth, and less flexibility in terms of tax-efficient accounting.

Table 2. Tax Lots by Fund Type

Type of Fund	Average Number of Lots	Average Position Breadth
Equity index	92	20%
Active equity	21	14
Fixed income	3	1
Separate account	Very few	Small

In contrast, fixed-income mutual funds have almost no ability to use accounting techniques because they typically have very few cost lots per security. Fixed-income funds thus tend to have few cost lots and very little breadth. For the average fixed-income fund, which has three cost lots and 1 percent breadth, whether to use HIFO or FIFO accounting is not an issue because the manager does not have much choice in terms of cost lots.

Separate accounts have a lot of flexibility in regard to the securities purchased and sold within a portfolio, but because they are often a one-time investment without sustained future cash flows, they tend to have very few cost lots and little position breadth. Accordingly, accounting strategies tend to have a much more powerful effect in the mutual fund context, whereas in separate accounts, trading strategies (such as harvesting losses, which is discussed below) must be used more heavily to improve tax efficiency.

Accounting does not affect pretax return. Accounting simply determines how to account for selling a security. Accounting does not recommend selling a security because of a tax reason.

Trading Strategies. Generally, trading strategies can be used much more effectively on the separate account side to affect after-tax returns. Trading strategies can affect pretax return for mutual funds, but they also come with trade-offs. In the end, trading strategies offer no guarantee of getting the desired result.

One obvious trading strategy is to maintain low turnover in the portfolio. Turnover, however, is an imperfect indicator of tax efficiency, as already discussed.

Another strategy is to focus on the tax cost of trading decisions. A portfolio may have a position in a stock that has a tremendous amount of unrealized gain, but the manager may no longer like the prospects of this stock and may want to replace it with something else. In addition to the other transaction costs, the manager has to recognize the tax cost of selling the position. The new position must have an expected return high enough to offset the tax cost.

Another consideration is loss harvesting, which involves opportunistically selling positions at a loss and using the loss to offset gains or, in the mutual fund context, carry the loss forward. The trade-off is that the ability to deduct the loss is constrained by the IRS wash sale rule, which states that an investor generally cannot realize the loss on the sale of a stock if the same stock is purchased within 30 days before or after the sale.

Another trade-off is how to explain to shareholders that because of variability in the stock market, the tax-managed fund may be less tax efficient in some periods than some tax-inefficient vehicles, or vice versa. Because of variability in the stock market, the best intentions may go awry.

Whether the manager is selling winners or losers makes a big difference in the tax efficiency of the portfolio. For example, consider the distinction between value and growth stocks. If a value manager buys a stock that is having some trouble and the stock continues to decline, the manager may choose to buy more of the stock if the fundamentals remain favorable and the stock decline is temporary. Alternatively, the manager may choose to realize the loss and buy the stock back after the wash sale period ends. Each choice has different implications for overall tax efficiency and the portfolio's return. Again, the real measure of tax efficiency is not pretax return but maximizing after-tax return.

Portfolio Construction. Using certain techniques in portfolio construction, such as emphasizing low dividend yields or using municipal bonds where appropriate, can make the portfolio more tax efficient.

Cash Flow Stability. Positive cash flow is good because it dilutes any unrealized gains in the fund (assuming equity prices rise over time) and also provides greater ability to use tax-efficient accounting methods in the future. Negative cash flow that is uncorrelated with stock market movements can be a bad thing. Market timing shareholders can ruin the tax management of a mutual fund. If a large portion of the fund is suddenly liquidated because of market timers, the effect on the remaining shareholders is negative. So, tax-managed mutual funds typically require high minimums and have high redemption fees. The redemption fee is justified for two reasons: First, it keeps out short-term investors, and second, the ones who leave pay the remaining shareholders—because redemption fees go back to the fund—for the potential tax cost that leaving the fund will impose on them.

Mutual Funds versus Separate Accounts

In evaluating the relative tax efficiency of mutual funds and separate accounts, this section focuses on cash flow and tax differences and concludes with a simulated comparison based on historical market data.

Cash Flow. Cash flow is at the crux of the debate over mutual funds versus separate accounts. The argument is that cash flow is usually bad. Mutual fund investors buy into an unrealized capital gain position and lose control over their own tax situation because of the actions of other shareholders in the fund. Furthermore, mutual funds commingle investors of different tax situations (e.g., taxable and tax-deferred). Certainly, negative cash flow can cause gain realizations, but focusing on the problems associated with negative cash flow overlooks the considerable benefits of both positive and negative cash flow.

Will sales result in realized gains for other shareholders? Although the usual answer is "yes," a more accurate answer is "possibly." Cash flow generally provides the portfolio manager with a tax-free rebalance. If a manager who needs to rebalance the portfolio has positive cash flow, the manager does not have to sell something else to generate the cash to buy a desired stock. Instead, the manager can redirect the cash flow to purchase the new securities. In such instances, positive cash flow provides a significant benefit.

■ *Negative cash flow.* Redemptions are not necessarily bad when the account management is tax sensitive because the HIFO accounting technique can be very powerful. The effect depends on why the redemptions have occurred. Consider how a 20 percent market downturn would affect a fund that does not use tax management and that has unrealized gains equal to 40 percent of its total assets. If the fund subsequently experienced massive redemptions, long-term investors would be saddled with the capital gains of short-term investors who are getting out because of the market drop. Of course, one positive side effect is that the market downturn would reduce the portfolio's level of unrealized capital gains.

On the other hand, a fund using tax-efficient accounting will realize the losses in a position before the gain. In a market downturn, all of a sudden, the fund has a lot more losses to realize. In fact, a market downturn is not the scenario in which a tax-efficient mutual fund will perform poorly; the portfolio will realize considerable losses that can be used to offset future capital gain realizations. The scenario in which a tax-efficient fund could eventually realize gains is when redemptions occur in a flat or rising market. If such conditions last long enough, the fund will have eaten through all of the losses in the position and will eventually be able to realize only gains.

This accounting difference can be powerful. Consider, for example, a large index fund with total assets of about $90 billion. Unrealized gains account for a whopping 41 percent of the fund's assets, which is a big tax liability according to many. Assume that a 20 percent market decline occurs and that the fund has a redemption of $10 billion, which is a little bit more than 10 percent of the fund's assets. Using FIFO accounting, the remaining shareholders would be hit with an 8 percent realized capital gain yield.

Consider the same fund with HIFO accounting. A 20 percent decline would require redemptions of $31.6 billion, or 44 percent of the fund's assets, before the first dollar of net gain would be realized. For a comparison of scale, note that during the market downturn of 1987, the fund used in this example experienced about 6 percent of assets redeemed in about a two-week period. So, 44 percent of the fund's assets is a huge redemption. In fact, anything less than a 44 percent redemption would actually realize net losses, which is a tax benefit to the remaining shareholders.

Similarly, even in a flat market, because the fund's cash flow would have created great position breadth and not every stock would be at its all-time high, the fund could experience redemption activity equal to 15 percent of total assets—$13.5 billion—without realizing any net gains. Even in a flat or rising market, 15 percent would represent a significant hit for the fund. This fund is not even tax managed. In the tax-managed version of this fund, the threshold for a flat market is 27 percent of total assets and the threshold for a 20 percent market decline is actually 83 percent. The explanation for such high thresholds is that some realized losses are already built up in the fund.

■ *Positive cash flow.* Positive cash flow is a significant benefit because a rising market dilutes any capital gains in a portfolio. If a mutual fund has an unrealized capital gain of 40 percent, new shareholders, who come in at current basis (if market value equals the current basis), dilute the capital gains position of the overall portfolio because new shareholders are coming in at, say, $100 a share on stock ABC, but the rest of the ABC positions might be at $70 a share. This dilution gives the investment manager more flexibility to choose higher cost lots, thereby lowering the taxable gain and raising the after-tax return if shareholders end up selling.

Tax Differences. From the investor's perspective, three major (and probably many minor) differences exist between the taxation of separate accounts and mutual funds. Two of the differences are disadvantages for the mutual fund and one is a significant advantage for the mutual fund.

First, in the separate account, net realized losses flow through to the shareholder, so the investor can use the losses as a deduction for the current tax year. In mutual funds, net losses cannot flow through to shareholders. Mutual funds are constrained to distribute nothing if they have a net loss; they can only use losses to offset capital gains and thus lower the capital gains distribution of the portfolio. Based on the time value of money, investors would rather have the loss today in the separate account to offset gains in other parts of their portfolios or to offset up to $3,000 of taxable income. This difference puts mutual funds at a disadvantage relative to separate accounts. Ultimately, the magnitude of the difference depends on the investor's tax situation.

Second, short-term gains in the separate account are reported on Schedule D (Capital Gain and Loss). Of course, realizing a lot of short-term gains is not very tax efficient. Mutual fund tax rules, however, were written so that short-term gains flow through as interest and dividend income for tax purposes, so they are reported on Schedule B (Interest and Dividends), not Schedule D. As such, short-term gains in mutual funds cannot be used directly to offset short-term losses. Consider an investor with long-term gains and short-term losses, as well as a short-term gain from a mutual fund. Short-term gains have a higher marginal effective tax rate than long-term gains. So, rather than using the short-term loss to offset long-term gains, such an investor would prefer to report the short-term gain on Schedule D in order to offset it with the short-term loss. For a tax-sensitive investor, however, this is not likely to be a major concern because they would tend to seek out funds that do not distribute a lot of short-term gains, which are highly tax inefficient.

The one major advantage of mutual funds is the deductibility of investment advisory expenses, which does not exist in the separate account world. Investment advisory expenses are normally subject to the 2 percent itemized deduction floor—that is, 2 percent of adjusted gross income—when itemizing deductions. In mutual funds, however, all expenses are deducted from the dividend yield of the fund. So, a mutual fund shareholder receives a net dividend distribution that reflects gross dividends minus expenses, which means a taxable shareholder is able to deduct all of the expenses of the fund. A 50 basis-point (bp) investment-advisory expense that cannot be deducted outside of the mutual fund versus one that is effectively deducted within the mutual fund means a difference—for a high-tax-bracket investor—of 40 percent of 20 bps a year. In terms of the tax advantages of a separate account versus the mutual fund, the deductibility of investment advisory expenses may offset the disadvantages of not being able to use net losses in the current tax year and having short-term gains reported as interest and dividends.

The question of overall tax efficiency, however, is more complex than simply examining tax differences. Separate accounts have three major disadvantages in regard to tax efficiency: locked-in positions, reliance on trading techniques, and a higher ratio (relative to mutual funds) of market value to cost basis when forced sales occur.

First, although separate accounts are highly tax efficient in the short run, over the long term, without the positive effects of cash flow, tax considerations can—possibly but not necessarily—paralyze portfolio management. That is, managers get locked into positions and are unable to rebalance portfolios without either new cash flow or generating significant gains.

For example, when America Online was added to the S&P 500 at the end of 1998, the problem was how to get AOL into an indexed portfolio. A mutual fund could have used current positive cash flow to buy the AOL position, or it could have used HIFO accounting by selling positions to generate the cash to buy the AOL position, probably realizing losses, as demonstrated by the example of flat and rising market redemption.

In separate accounts, managers had a couple of choices. They could have sold positions to raise the cash to buy AOL. If the account began at year-end 1994 without much further cash flow, however, it would have experienced a great increase in value since inception. As a result, managers had little ability, if any, to get AOL into the portfolio without realizing a lot of gain. The alternative would have been not adding AOL or adding it in an under-weighted position and accepting some tracking error relative to the index. Over time, as an account gets older, such considerations become more serious because the account's positions become increasingly locked in, which means repeatedly choosing between accepting tracking error or realizing gains in order to add a new stock to the portfolio.

Second, separate accounts must rely more on trading techniques, such as loss harvesting, to maintain tax efficiency. For reasons already discussed in this presentation, the main problem with relying on trading techniques is that their success is highly uncertain, and unlike the use of accounting techniques, they require the manager to assess a trade-off between pretax return and tax efficiency.

The final potential disadvantage of separate accounts is that the ratio of market value to cost basis is higher when a forced sale occurs, as in M&A activity. Buy and hold is a popular strategy, but it is not fail-safe. I am currently writing a paper on this strategy.[2] The research looks at the 50 largest stocks as of year-end 1983. Of those 50 largest stocks, 7 no longer exist. Six of these seven stocks were involved in mergers that would have been taxable events for shareholders. So, managers who prefer not to sell may be forced to sell as a result of M&A activity.

A Simulated Comparison. To evaluate the relative tax efficiency of mutual funds and separate accounts, consider the example of a simulated open-end S&P 500 index fund and a closed-end fund of the same type, which is a proxy for a separate account—in other words, this example compares a fund with cash flow and a fund with no cash flow. **Table 3** shows the results of research based on simulations using data from August 1, 1976, through December 31, 1991.[3] Both funds are tax managed. That is, they try to harvest losses wherever possible and maintain as little tracking error as possible versus the S&P 500.

In the first five years, neither the open-end nor the closed-end fund realized a gain. In fact, because 1981 was not a great year in the market, both the open-end variant and the closed-end variant had a significant loss carryforward and both funds had virtually equal amounts of unrealized capital gains.

In Year 11 through Year 15, the open-end fund still had not realized a gain because it took advantage of simple tax-management techniques. In fact, the

[2]Joel M. Dickson, John B. Shoven, and Clemens Sialm, "Tax Externalities of Equity Mutual Funds," *National Tax Journal* (forthcoming).

[3]Joel M. Dickson and John B. Shoven, "A Stock Index Mutual Fund without Net Capital Gains Realizations," Working Paper 4717, National Bureau of Economic Research (April 1994).

Table 3. Comparison of Simulated Open-End and Closed-End S&P 500 Index Funds

	Open-End Simulation[a]			Closed-End Simulation		
Years	Average Realized Gain (% NAV)	Ending Loss Carryover (% assets)	Ending Net Unrealized Gain (% assets)	Average Realized Gain (% NAV)	Ending Loss Carryover (% assets)	Ending Net Unrealized Gain (% assets)
1–5	0.0%	6.4%	22.6%	0.0%	10.1%	25.0%
6–10	0.0	0.5	35.8	0.02	0.0	52.9
11–15	0.0	5.3	29.5	1.1	1.7	63.2

Note: NAV = net asset value.

[a] Open-end simulation used monthly cash flow data from The Vanguard Group's 500 Index Fund.

open-end fund finished this period with a loss carryover of 5.3 percent and, as a result, could continue to be tax efficient well into the future. The open-end portfolio had an unrealized gain position of about 29.5 percent, which was significant but nothing like the unrealized capital gain position of 63.2 percent in the closed-end variant. The high level of unrealized gains in the closed-end fund occurred because the fund had no cash flow and its entire 15-year history was in a rising market.

On the other hand, the average gain in the closed-end variant was 1.1 percentage points of net asset value over the period from Year 11 through Year 15. The closed-end fund ended with a loss carryover because the final year of the period was 1991 and the market downturn in 1990 provided the opportunity to realize some losses. So, in the final year of the simulation, the closed-end variant was able to offset its losses with gains and have a little bit of loss left over. As shown in Table 3 for Year 6 through Year 15, the closed-end fund, using a low-turnover approach and tax-management techniques, generated very small amounts of realized gain and ended the period with more unrealized gains than the open-end fund. The open-end fund, in which the cash flow provided greater flexibility for using tax-management techniques, realized no gains for the entire period and ended the period with a significant loss carryover. Little difference in tracking error existed between these two portfolios.

In mutual funds, the cash flow offers the flexibility to use the accounting techniques that can erase about 80–85 percent of the realized gains in this type of index fund. Because these techniques can minimize the bulk of the realized gains, the manager does not have to worry about tracking error; the gains will not affect pretax return. Thus, the fund gets the best of both worlds—tight tracking and excellent tax efficiency.

Conclusion

In contrast to conventional wisdom, mutual funds can be very tax-efficient management structures. Portfolio management and tax considerations can be integrated, and accounting techniques can be powerful tools in managing taxable events. The usual argument against mutual funds being tax-efficient vehicles focuses almost exclusively on the supposed problems associated with negative cash flow and ignores the significant benefits of positive cash flow. Furthermore, portfolio managers and management companies can use certain practices to mitigate the potential tax liability of negative cash flow. The introduction of so-called tax-managed funds in the past several years is only the beginning of a trend. These funds are still a small part of the overall industry, representing less than 1 percent of assets, but in about 30–35 portfolios, the focus is on after-tax return.

Greater segmentation will likely occur among equity mutual funds, with different vehicles for clients with taxable assets and for those with tax-exempt or tax-deferred assets. Given that mutual funds can be tax efficient, mutual funds represent an opportunity—even for high-net-worth investors—to achieve good diversification within the context of an overall tax-efficient plan.

Question and Answer Session

Joel M. Dickson

Question: Have any studies compared historical tax efficiency with expected future tax efficiency?

Dickson: Some studies have looked at whether past tax efficiency predicts future tax efficiency, and they tend to show that past tax efficiency is a slightly better predictor than pretax return. These studies, however, looked at preliquidation calculations, so a trade-off is involved. The fact that investors received lower distributions along the road means that they probably have a higher tax liability in the end, when they sell the position. Deferring taxes as long as possible is still the name of the game. Daniel Bergstresser and James Poterba from MIT have written an excellent paper on this topic.[1]

Question: Does the Morningstar database provide reliable information on accounting practices, particularly with respect to embedded gains?

Dickson: The Morningstar database gives information on the current unrealized capital gain position of the fund. This statistic, like turnover, is an imperfect predictor of tax efficiency because it does not give information on the accounting procedure, and different accounting procedures can make a big difference in potential tax liability. Mutual funds usually do not disclose accounting practices—the average telephone representative of a mutual fund company has no idea what a particular fund's accounting practices

are. Maybe they should, especially during periods when investors might be worried about accounting practices, such as when redemption activity is severe.

Question: Using the Morningstar data on tax efficiency, can you determine how much of a fund's tax efficiency is attributable, over time, to accounting techniques, trading techniques, or cash flow (e.g., deposits and redemptions)?

Dickson: The quick answer is no, but this question brings up an important point. Consider the factors that can affect tax efficiency. An after-tax return number or a tax efficiency number tells you how the compilation of the roughly 30–40 different factors that could affect tax efficiency actually worked. This presentation discusses only five factors (investment strategy, character of portfolio holdings, turnover strategy, accounting procedures, and shareholder activity). Many other factors could affect tax efficiency as well. Breaking overall tax efficiency into the separate components is extremely difficult because the process is integrated, which is why evaluating tax efficiency is so complicated.

Question: Does The Vanguard Group, or any other fund family, use tax efficiency as an element in fund manager compensation, and if not, will the use of tax efficiency become more prevalent in the future?

Dickson: Again, the short answer is no. In fact, in the prospectuses for all of our actively managed funds, we state that the portfolio is generally not managed with regard to tax ramifications, so

buyer beware. Our managers are generally compensated according to how they perform on a pretax basis relative to a pretax benchmark. In our tax-managed funds, prospectuses say we strive for after-tax return.

Compensation on an after-tax basis is likely to become a reality. The problem is that constructing after-tax market benchmarks is difficult. The only competitor benchmarks in the mutual fund world are those provided by data services, such as Morningstar. The question remains, relative to market benchmarks, what is the after-tax return on the S&P 500? The answer depends on when the portfolio started, so people think of the S&P 500 as a series. The S&P 500 portfolio that started in 1994 had a certain after-tax return in 1999, but the one that started in 1996 might have a different after-tax return in 1999 because of changes to the index that affect capital gains realizations. Once people figure out a good way to do after-tax market benchmarking, after-tax manager compensation will be feasible.

Question: How many mutual funds are currently using some form of tax-sensitive accounting, such as HIFO, and is such accounting becoming more generally used or not?

Dickson: Tax-sensitive accounting is becoming widely used; it is relatively easy to use and does not give up anything in pretax return. Exact numbers are unavailable because funds do not disclose what tax accounting methods they use or the extent to which other tax-management techniques are used.

---

[1] Daniel Bergstresser and James Poterba, "Do After-Tax Returns Affect Mutual Fund Inflows?," Working Paper 7595, National Bureau of Economic Research (March 2000).

Question: Do you expect to see more mutual funds offering tax-managed and non-tax-managed versions of their funds because trying to optimize both is inefficient, and if so, will the pretax returns of tax-managed and non-tax-managed clones differ much?

Dickson: The industry is heading in this direction. Unfortunately, this approach has a little bit of a marketing tinge. Because of the commingling of pretax and after-tax investors in the typical equity mutual fund, you can make an economic argument that you would rather be in a fund as an after-tax investor with other after-tax investors so that all of the tax interests would be aligned. Similarly, in a fund managed for an IRA or 401(k) plan, having only pretax investors is preferable in order to prevent the manager from thinking about the tax consequences of managing the portfolio.

The pretax returns for mutual funds can vary a lot as a function of the variability in the equity market. Furthermore, pretax return depends on cash flow, tax-management practices, and many other factors. Differences in cash flow alone could cause pretax return to differ significantly among clone funds.

Question: How does the tax efficiency of SPDRs (Standard & Poor's Depositary Receipts) and other index-participation unit investment trusts compare with the tax efficiency of mutual funds, such as index funds?

Dickson: SPDRs have been fairly efficient. They distributed gains in 1996 but not in the past couple of years. SPDRs have generally avoided some gain realizations by redeeming shareholders with stock rather than cash. The prospectuses of SPDRs describe how they use this approach. This technique, however, is not unique to SPDRs: It is also available to mutual funds.

SPDRs have lost a bit less to taxes than traditional index funds, such as Vanguard's 500 Index Fund. SPDRs, however, have generated a lower pretax return because of the various structures of the unit investment trust. For example, they can reinvest dividend distributions only on a periodic basis, and they can't invest in futures. As a result of these limitations, SPDRs have had a little bit of a cash drag in a generally rising equity market. So, although SPDRs have lost less to taxes than the 500 Index Fund, they have had a lower after-tax return.

That said, investors can get good tax management without having to invest in the exchange-traded funds. For example, our Tax-Managed Growth & Income Fund has not distributed any capital gains since its inception five years ago. SPDRs actually distributed capital gains during this period. So, a mutual fund was able to achieve both good tax efficiency and excellent tracking with the S&P 500.

The new exchange-traded funds that are coming out are set up as mutual funds, not as unit investment trusts. As such, they have more flexibility to invest in assets such as futures and can avoid the cash drag that the SPDRs have (although that drag is small). These vehicles will probably offer good tax efficiency and good tracking. Nevertheless, tax-managed mutual funds can get similar performance by using simple procedures, such as HIFO accounting and loss harvesting. Comparing SPDRs and other exchange-traded products with a regular index fund is like comparing apples and oranges. Tax-sensitive investors should probably look for a tax-managed vehicle.

Question: Although mutual funds can be tax efficient within themselves, if investment managers use multiple funds instead of multiple separate accounts to achieve asset allocation, do they lose the opportunity to do active tax management among different asset classes for individual clients?

Dickson: Investment managers have to decide how to rebalance portfolios in a taxable environment. Rebalancing with mutual funds is different from using separate accounts only to the extent that managers can move assets around in the separate account. For stocks, the answer is maybe—if the manager does a little bit more in the separate account. For changing asset allocations in stocks, bonds, and cash, managers still have the problem of how to do it. Managers can do more security identification with separate accounts. Instead of selling a certain stock mutual fund, they can sell a position in a depreciated security; doing so lowers the stock weighting and provides a tax benefit. Certainly, this potential benefit requires a lot of management on the investor's part, unless all of the separate accounts are in one place and run by one person.

Question: Because the tax-sensitive manager is only as good as his or her custodian's tax sensitivity, which is generally poor, will custodians update their systems to use HIFO accounting?

Dickson: Yes, many mutual fund companies have their own internal accounting systems, so changing to HIFO accounting is easy. Managers for high-net-worth individuals have had to deal with tax efficiency for a long time and have the necessary systems in place. Mutual funds have a lot of flexibility in their existing accounting systems.

Question: What is the potential for changes in U.S. tax laws that would give managers more flexibility to distribute rather than invest realized gains?

Dickson: Managers have some flexibility now and can choose not to distribute capital gains. Technically, the only requirement for mutual funds is to distribute 90 percent of their net investment income, which does not include long-term capital gains. So, managers could reinvest realized gains in a fund. Doing so would subject the fund's shareholders to corporate taxation on those gains, and as anyone would realize, you would rather pass gains to the shareholders than have them pay the corporate tax.

I see potential for changing the tax law requiring mutual fund investors to report short-term gains on Schedule B (Interest and Dividends). Some debate has arisen recently about whether mutual funds are really pass-through entities. If so, the laws should probably be fixed to allow short-term gains to flow through so that investors can report them on Schedule D, as with other types of investments.

Question: Why do you think small-cap mutual funds are not as tax efficient as large-cap funds, given that the need to minimize tracking error is less critical in the small-cap area and that M&A activity is more prevalent in the large-cap area?

Dickson: M&A activity is more prevalent in the small-cap area. In large-cap stocks, M&A activity often consists of tax-free stock swaps. In small-cap stocks, cash deals often occur that are taxable events for the shareholder. For example, consider Johnson & Johnson's take over of Centocor. Small-cap funds holding Centocor suddenly got undesired exposure to Johnson & Johnson, a large-cap stock that many small-cap managers would be forced to sell to maintain their portfolios' character. Although the acquisition might have been tax free, it was not tax free for those small-cap managers who ended up selling Johnson & Johnson out of the portfolio. Because small-cap stocks tend to grow out of their universe, more opportunity exists for tax management to add value in the small-cap area.

Question: Rather than segmenting or using specialized equity funds in their portfolios, should taxable investors use general funds so that managers are not restricted to selling off issues that move out of their style box?

Dickson: Yes, one of the best ways to hold small-cap stocks is within the context of an overall total portfolio. If you're holding the Wilshire 5000 and a small-cap stock becomes first a mid-cap and then a large-cap stock, the stock is still in the Wilshire 5000 and you're not forced to hold an inappropriate stock. Similarly, holding a generic core portfolio that is not necessarily size or style specific is a way to achieve broad diversification and better tax management within the portfolio context.

Tax-Aware Equity Investing

Jean L.P. Brunel, CFA
CEO
Winter Capital Consulting, LLC[1]

Passive index investing is often touted for its tax efficiency, but it has serious limitations. The key to providing superior tax efficiency is an active strategy that incorporates tax-aware methods of security selection, portfolio construction, and risk management. Although optimum tax efficiency may be highly difficult to achieve, managers can use a straightforward analytical framework to produce acceptable results.

Many investors believe that indexing and passive management offer the only reliable approach to tax-managed investing. This solution, however, is incomplete at best. This presentation examines the shortcomings of passive management and explains why active management, which can mean both active security selection and active tax management, is potentially superior for the construction of tax-aware portfolios. Furthermore, achieving the desired level of tax efficiency does not absolutely require the use of active strategies that depend on complicated information technology to produce results. Investment managers can provide good tax management by using a relatively simple analytical framework that allows them to evaluate tax issues in security selection, portfolio construction, and risk management.

Indexing and Passive Management

Two myths are important when considering the tax efficiency of indexing and passive management. First, many investors believe that indexing is the easy solution to tax-efficient investing. Second, many investors believe a passive approach to investing is more tax efficient than an active approach. Neither belief, however, is necessarily correct.

Indexing. Indexing is popular because it offers a number of advantages. In contrast to an active approach, it usually has lower management costs, lower tracking error, and lower administrative costs (both in terms of time and dollars). Unfortunately,

indexing also has disadvantages. It offers no scope for security-selection alpha or for tax-management alpha.

Passive Management. When considering a passive-management approach, such as indexing, investors should think critically about their decision. This is because the active–passive debate often confuses the debate on tax-efficient investing. One problem is knowing what "passive" and "active" actually mean. Some passive funds execute a systematic replication of the index, which means that the portfolio holds a proportional exposure to every single stock in the index. Other passive investing techniques, such as sampling, provide relatively low expected tracking error and do not require a change in the whole portfolio every time a stock is added to or dropped from an index because of a merger or otherwise. The issue revolves around the following observation: By "active," most people mean focusing on security-selection alpha; seeking *tax-management alpha*, however, may also be considered an active strategy.

Few managers consistently beat the index in the 1990s. The past five years have been exceptional for large-cap stocks, and portfolio managers who were not invested in large-cap stocks with a growth bias were doomed to underperform the index. The market capitalization of the average holding of the average manager in the Morningstar universe, or in any other universe for that matter, tends to be lower than the market cap of the average stock in the index. As a result, managers have done poorly for the past five years because the key to producing the best-performing portfolio has been to overweight the 50 largest-cap stocks in the index. In an environment in

---

[1]Mr. Brunel is now at First American Asset Management, where he is the chief investment officer of the High-Net-Worth Group.

which small-cap or mid-cap stocks had performed well, active managers would probably have performed better.

Another source of distraction in the active–passive debate is tracking error. In the tax-oblivious world, risk and return are the only dimensions, and a basic article of faith is "Do not incur tracking error"—with tracking error meaning any difference in performance relative to the index—without having a reasonable expectation of gaining some alpha. The three-dimensional world of after-tax investing, however, includes risk, return, *and* taxes. Given the choice between two portfolios that produce roughly the same pretax return, one with 95 percent tax efficiency and a 2 percent tracking error and the other with 85 percent tax efficiency and a 1 percent tracking error, which one would a rational investor choose? The traditional answer, which would favor the low tracking error alternative, is not obviously the right one, and a higher tracking error might be a small price to pay for gaining the higher after-tax return. The point is that the idea of avoiding tracking error at all costs does not necessarily make sense.

Traditional active managers will hardly ever do better than passive managers over any long period of time; active managers *are* the universe and the universe cannot be expected to outperform itself when the universe is being tagged with management fees and the index is not. Over the long term, only about one manager in three outperforms the index on a pretax basis. Recently, the ratio has been about 1 manager in 10, which may be an extreme aberration.

Given such performance data, the issue of tax management becomes even more important than security selection. Major volatility in a market provides a huge opportunity to take losses without incurring any significant tracking error against the index and thus without underperforming the index. For example, when drug stocks fell in 1992, managers with a loss in Merck & Company could sell it and buy Pfizer, thereby trading one stock for the other without a significant difference in the portfolio's exposure to industry risk factors.

The strategy referred to as "passive structured," in which the focus is on managing taxes rather than managing securities, addresses such volatility issues. David Stein and Premkumar Narasimhan recently examined this strategy in an article published in the *Journal of Private Portfolio Management*. A simulation reported in this article indicates that, in the U.S. equity market, the potential exists for an annual 1.6 percent alpha coming from tax reduction alone.[2] In

other words, a portfolio can track an index and produce 1.6 percent of value in tax losses that can be used to offset realized capital gains elsewhere in the portfolio. This accomplishment is notable in terms of added value. Thus, passive-structured management is in fact an active strategy, one in which the focus is on active tax management rather than active security selection.

An Analytical Framework

The framework I use to analyze tax efficiency in portfolio construction allows managers either to observe their own processes or, as they recommend investments to clients, to analyze how other managers manage money. The main principle is that tax efficiency reflects the interaction of three critical variables: security selection, portfolio construction, and risk management.

Security Selection. Security selection is the process through which investment opportunities are selected. Two areas of security selection have great significance for tax efficiency: defining the investment universe and deciding how to perform investment research.

First, to understand the importance of defining the investment universe, consider a simple situation in which a manager is handling a portfolio of large-cap U.S. equities. The manager can think of the investment universe in two ways. One method, the "raw" approach, is to decide that all stocks in the S&P 500 Index, and maybe a few additional stocks at the periphery, are eligible for inclusion in the portfolio and are thus part of the universe. An alternative method is to screen stocks for certain characteristics that may enhance their tax efficiency. For example, holdings with long expected investment horizons tend to be more tax efficient because they require less short-term turnover, which puts the return on capital for such stocks in the 20 percent rather than 40 percent tax bracket.

The second area of security selection, how the manager actually performs investment research, is a neglected subject. I have yet to see an article that compares the relative benefits of doing investment research on a pretax basis versus an after-tax basis, and as far as I know, no one seems to have done serious research on whether using an after-tax dividend discount model makes sense. Thus, the investment research process raises significant tax-efficiency issues. For example, is the research done with the purpose of forecasting expected after-tax or pretax returns? The difference could have serious tax implications for investors. Is the research qualitative or quantitative? Although quantitative research has

---

[2] David Stein and Premkumar Narasimhan, "Of Passive and Active Equity Portfolios in the Presence of Taxes," *Journal of Private Portfolio Management* (Fall 1999):55–63.

many advantages in terms of both management costs and repeatability, one major disadvantage is that no one can make an accurate model of reality.

Portfolio Construction. Portfolio construction is simply the process through which individual buy and sell decisions are made. With the exception of tax-loss harvesting, portfolio construction guidelines for tax-aware investing are not significantly different from what would be done on a pretax basis.

Unfortunately, because most portfolios do not have significant positive cash flow during the course of the year, buying one security usually means selling another to pay for the purchase. In a tax-oblivious portfolio, every transaction a portfolio manager makes is meant to generate alpha in the form of either additional return or lower risk for the same return. For those who manage money on an after-tax basis, the expected alpha associated with the transaction is a function of both the excess return that is expected from the purchased stock versus the sold stock and the cost from the realized gain on the sold stock. In short, the threshold excess return needed to make a transaction worthwhile is inversely proportional to the amount of unrealized gain in the security that is to be sold.

To make transactions more efficient, managers can use "alpha-enabling" transactions. In an alpha-enabling transaction, a manager takes a loss in a security, invests in a security that is equivalent or almost equivalent, and uses the loss generated to offset the gain in yet another transaction, thereby giving the overall transaction a reasonable expected alpha. By doing so, the manager generates an alpha that would not exist otherwise.

Tax issues are equally as important as stock selection in the portfolio construction process. Tax-aware managers should use systematic loss harvesting. This method is based on the principle that a loss in a portfolio is a free option to take a gain now or at some future point. It allows managers to rebalance portfolios, either within an asset class or among asset classes, when a portfolio has drifted away from the strategic asset allocation.

Risk Management. Risk management, the third and final dimension of the framework, is the process through which a list of holdings becomes a portfolio. Two issues in this area are important for tax management. First, despite what many managers think, tracking error is not necessarily best when it is minimized. Few managers realize that tracking error is a cost that can be offset by alpha or tax efficiency.

Second, setting industry weights or sector constraints simply to look like a particular index often places arbitrary restrictions on portfolios. Certain managers have designed portfolios to minimize tracking error with a given index without first bothering to check whether the index is relevant to the client's situation. Managers could actually adopt modified and better-suited reference indexes without necessarily hurting their clients over time, particularly if those indexes have long-term expected returns that approximate the broad market while avoiding certain tax-inefficient sectors.

The Three-Dimensional Framework. A framework with three axes is a good way to look at tax-efficient equity management, as shown in **Figure 1**. The axes—which represent the three dimensions of the framework: security selection, risk management, and portfolio construction—range not from zero to infinity but from tax oblivious to tax sensitive. A tax-

Figure 1. A Three-Dimensional Analytical Framework for Tax-Aware Portfolio Construction

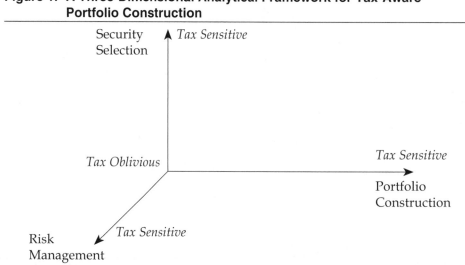

oblivious manager, with a portfolio represented by a point at the origin (i.e., where all three axes intersect), does not care about taxes or at least has no direct focus on taxes. A tax-sensitive manager, represented by a point with coordinates near the end of each axis, takes taxes fully into account in every single decision.

Tax-Aware Portfolio Construction

In regard to tax efficiency, the two extremes (ranging from least to greatest tax sensitivity) among the various approaches to portfolio construction are tax oblivious and passive structured.[3] Between these

[3]For a discussion of the passive-structured process, see Mr. Stein's presentation in this proceedings

extremes are five generic approaches: the traditional tax-managed process, goal-based tax efficiency, screen-based tax efficiency, systematic tax efficiency, and integrated tax efficiency. **Figure 2** shows how these five approaches look on the three-dimensional framework of tax management. (In Figure 2, the dot in each panel shows how a given process ranks on each of the three axes.)

Traditional Tax-Managed Process. The traditional tax-managed process has been adopted by a number of mutual fund companies that want to be able to offer tax-managed portfolios or at least label certain portfolios as tax managed. In doing so, however, these companies offer only two significant differences, as shown in Panel A of Figure 2. First, these

Figure 2. Comparison of Different Methods of Tax-Aware Portfolio Construction

A. Traditional Tax-Managed Process

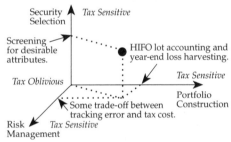

D. Systematic Tax Efficiency

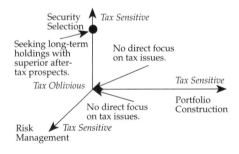

B. Goal-Based Tax Efficiency

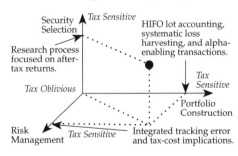

E. Integrated Tax Efficiency

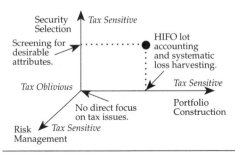

C. Screen-Based Tax Efficiency

tax-managed funds use the HIFO (highest in/first out) approach for lot accounting, which has a significant impact on tax efficiency. Second, these funds use year-end loss harvesting.

Goal-Based Tax Efficiency. In goal-based tax efficiency, the portfolio manager selects a limited number of securities for which the expected holding period is very long or the expected return is extremely high. For example, one manager I know tries to invest in the "gazelles" of an industry, which are the firms that are taking market share away from the industry's "dinosaurs," because he thinks the gazelle stocks will double, triple, or quadruple in value. On a normal day, his portfolio consists of 10–30 stocks, but the gazelles are a majority. As shown in Panel B of Figure 2, managers who use this approach effectively ignore portfolio construction, tax implications with respect to selling securities or harvesting losses, and risk management (because no benchmark is used). Instead, they concentrate entirely on seeking stocks with long-term potential.

Screen-Based Tax Efficiency. Screen-based tax efficiency differs in the sense that the manager screens for stocks with desirable attributes. For example, a manager might use four screens. Three of the screens might be considered style neutral but would look for stocks with long-term growth potential. One screen could have a value orientation, which would allow the manager to acquire value stocks that are too cheap to ignore. As shown in Panel C of Figure 2, a screen-based portfolio construction process uses not only HIFO accounting and systematic loss harvesting; it also has buy and sell disciplines that focus on a net positive after-tax alpha. In terms of risk management, a screen-based process has no specific focus on the interaction between tracking error and tax efficiency.

Systematic Tax Efficiency. Systematic tax efficiency is arguably the best practical approach available. The manager uses the same kind of portfolio construction process as the one described for screen-based portfolio construction, but as shown in Panel D of Figure 2, the manager also uses some form of risk management to ensure that tracking error is allowed when the portfolio produces higher tax efficiency and disallowed when it does not.

Integrated Tax Efficiency. Integrated tax efficiency is the tax efficiency dream. Achieving this ideal level is possible, but it involves a complex research process focused on after-tax results. As shown in Panel E of Figure 2, this portfolio construction process uses alpha-enabling transactions, sys-

tematic loss harvesting, HIFO lot accounting, and a risk-management process, all of which are integrated in a risk model that evaluates the trade-off between tracking error and taxes.

Developing Systems for Tax Efficiency

Although the systematic and integrated approaches offer the best levels of tax efficiency, they require the use of expert systems that are difficult to apply for four main reasons.

First, managers have to make either an implicit or explicit quantitative forecast of the expected return of each security. Although managers care more about the relative ranking than the absolute value of the expected return on alternative investments, the reality is that on an after-tax basis, the absolute level of the return plays a significant role. Developing explicit return forecasts is extremely difficult, especially for extended periods of time.

Second, a wide disparity exists among the various risk models that are available to managers. In the U.S. equity market, tried-and-true models for small-cap stocks are available, but for other asset classes, such as emerging market equities, the quality of available risk models is uneven because they are still chiefly in a developmental phase.

Third, incorporating a portfolio manager's insights in a systematic fashion is extremely difficult. In one way or another, risk models are "mindless." The model may produce a supposedly optimal portfolio, but in reality, it may not be executed because it may not be sensible. Portfolio managers can play with the inputs to make the model reflect their own views, but doing so is difficult, in large measure because of the complexity of the models. In fact, if models were simpler, another problem could be exacerbated: If analysts can incorporate a portfolio manager's preferences or tendencies into the model, they can then game their forecasts to appeal to the manager. This possibility would eliminate, or at least diminish, the potential value of the analysts' perspective.

Finally, expert systems create enormous demand for information technology, which may exceed the capacity of many investment managers.

A screen-based approach to portfolio construction is easier to use than systematic or integrated methods and offers several advantages. Screening systems do not require explicit alpha forecasts or the use of risk models, and they are perfect for integrating a portfolio manager's insights. They nevertheless have significant disadvantages. They do not allow for adequate analysis with respect to the tax implication of any particular transaction, and they do not allow a portfolio manager to make a decent evaluation of the consequences of accepting tracking error. One way to deal with such shortcomings is to construct a process with the following steps.

Starting with a relevant equity universe, apply a set of both quantitative after-tax screens and insights from qualitative after-tax research to create an approved list of investment candidates. The word "approved" has various connotations in the investment management industry, but the point is to shrink the universe from 500 stocks to 200 stocks.

The next step of the process is to create a target portfolio with the use of certain analytical tools, not an integrated risk model. For example, a tool as simple as a swap analyzer can help the portfolio manager decide whether a trade makes sense or what kind of investment horizon is necessary for a trade to make sense, which would make the swap analyzer, in effect, an after-tax management tool. Risk–return management can be done by running a relatively simple risk model that looks at the expected tracking error of the portfolio relative to an index. Then, the issue becomes a matter of translating the target portfolio—the tax-oblivious portfolio—down to each individual client portfolio.

What makes the expert system process difficult is not so much the creation of an individual portfolio but rather the creation of many individual portfolios. An institution that manages more than 20 or 30 portfolios needs to be able to run every single portfolio through the expert system, which is a process that uses up an enormous amount of information technology capacity. Alternatively, comparing each individual client portfolio with a target is a much simpler process, and such an approach effectively incorporates implicit, as opposed to explicit, alpha forecasts. Managers can use such a system to track the deviation between the target portfolio and each client's portfolio and can incorporate tax-management issues relative to each client. For example, one of my clients generated a significant tax loss, which was completely unrelated to his financial assets, and did not need to worry about taxes for that year. This situation allowed us to refresh the bases of most securities in the client's portfolio without being concerned about the tax cost. Using a target portfolio allows investors to take advantage of such opportunities.

Conclusion

Managers who want to improve their own processes can achieve many of the advantages associated with integrated tax efficiency without using complex information technology. The solution is to use an analytical framework that recognizes the fundamental dimensions of tax-efficient portfolio construction and that allows managers to analyze the tax efficiency of their own portfolio construction process, as well as the processes used by others, in a consistent fashion. Such an approach may not be elegant or computerized, but when done correctly, it can achieve most of the critical objectives.

Question and Answer Session

Jean L.P. Brunel, CFA

Question: For a holding period longer than 12 months, does realizing short-term losses make sense, especially when the underlying securities are still a long way from becoming long term?

Brunel: You are better off when you can offset short-term losses against short-term gains. Using the short-term losses' overflow to offset against long-term gains costs some tax efficiency. On the other hand, consider the problem of buying a stock that you expect to hold for a long time but that increases sharply in value and is taken over by another company. In such a circumstance, my approach to taking losses is simple. You take a loss, unless a good reason justifies not doing so. I recommend that all my clients should have a Pavlovian response to taking losses. If the loss is bigger in percentage terms than the expected cost of buying and selling the security, the safe answer is to take the loss. Taking the loss may waste an investment opportunity, but a loss is a free option.

Question: Would you provide some practical examples of after-tax screens and qualitative research?

Brunel: Certain managers screen on both five-year earnings growth rates and five-year growth in sales per share. The difference between the two has to do with the belief that sales growth is an important determinant of future growth. Some managers believe in unit growth. A screen for earnings per share growth over a five-year period eliminates all Internet companies, but sales growth may still yield a few of these companies, so that screen focuses principally on

the growth part of the equation. Usually, at least one screen would include something to do with profitability, such as return on equity, return on assets, or operating margins.

Managers use screens to rank each security of the universe. So, if you have 500 securities, the securities will be ranked from 1 to 500 for each different screen. The screens may also be either equal weighted or weighted differently. In such a case, you sum the weighted scores of the securities on each screen to give you a z score for each security and then pick the top 200.

Some screens have a value tilt. Such screens may be used in an absolute sense, or they may be measured relative to the industry average in an attempt to avoid the industry bias that an absolute screen would create. Some managers use screens for price momentum, in which the idea is that you want privileged stocks whose prices have been going up (this avoids having to wait for a stock to be discovered). If you use the BARRA model, you can reflect momentum by placing a positive emphasis on the factor "success in the market."

Question: On a list of rank attractions of the universe, would the list be different if the rank attraction were after tax versus pretax? If you have two sets of portfolios, taxable and nontaxable, do you use the same universe list for each or is the rank attraction of your universe different for one versus the other?

Brunel: Conceptually, I would use different screens on an after-tax basis. For instance, the evidence clearly suggests that over

the long term, no significant difference exists in terms of returns for value or growth stocks. Yet, for a taxable investor, there is a difference: Value tends to have lower volatility and growth tends to have higher tax efficiency. If I followed a tax-oblivious strategy, I would want to have at least an equal weight on a screen for growth versus one for value; if I focused on after-tax returns, I would be comfortable having more weight on growth because over the long term, growth stocks tend to provide better after-tax returns.

Question: What is an acceptable tax-efficiency ratio for an actively managed portfolio?

Brunel: The average tax efficiency of the average large-cap universe (using the Morningstar after-tax return as the basis for the calculation) is slightly higher than 80 percent, which means that the implicit tax rate is slightly lower than 20 percent. For the value universe, the number drops to 75–78 percent, and a pure growth universe provides tax efficiency of 82–83 percent. An index fund in that same general environment provides about 95 percent tax efficiency. In an after-tax world, a fund should have a tax efficiency in excess of 90 percent. In the context of the overall portfolio, for an actively managed equity portfolio with 90–95 percent tax efficiency, some passive-structured exposure would have a tax efficiency in excess of 100 percent because the exposure would generate net tax losses. Achieving tax efficiency in, say, emerging market equities is extremely difficult, so investors interested in emerging market equities should expect tax inefficiency from such portfolios.

The main point is that for certain strategies, incorporating tax efficiency can improve the alpha enormously. But investors should consider why they want to hire a certain manager. If they want tax efficiency, then the manager's tax efficiency has to be at least 90 percent. If they want alpha, 70 percent tax efficiency is acceptable.

Question: Do you track the tax efficiencies of your firm's portfolios, and how do you determine whether they are achieving the 90 percent target?

Brunel: We track the tax efficiency of every manager, and the number is readily available. We look at the tax efficiency—defined as the ratio of after-tax to pretax returns—of the assets that we manage. We tend to focus on whether managers are true to what they have told us they would do. If we sense that a manager is doing something different, we will go to that manager and ask what is going on.

Question: Can you elaborate on your alpha-enabling transaction within the integrated tax-efficient model?

Brunel: Imagine a taxable portfolio that holds General Motors Corporation with a 50 percent capital gain and Merck with a loss. Based on analyst reports, the portfolio manager decides that Ford Motor Company is a better prospect than GM in terms of potential for excess return. At the same time, the manager decides that Merck and Pfizer are both likely to be average performers in the pharmaceutical industry over the next 3–5 years, so the manager can sell Merck and buy Pfizer without affecting the portfolio's risk–return expectations. This transaction, selling Merck and buying Pfizer, in itself, does not change the portfolio. The portfolio doesn't have a higher expected return, and it doesn't have any more volatility. Merck and Pfizer are even replacements for each other. But the loss in Merck can offset the gain in GM, which would allow the manager to have a portfolio that owns Ford and Pfizer rather than Merck and GM. The Pfizer-for-Merck transaction enables the manager to make the Ford-for-GM transaction, which would not have been possible otherwise.

Such an example, however, applies to stocks within the same country. Imagine a portfolio holding an emerging market fund at a loss and many U.S. stocks with gains. The portfolio manager would like to realize some of those gains but is concerned about the tax consequences. So, the manager develops an alpha-enabling transaction using the emerging market fund. Regardless of the mutual fund family, many emerging market funds have roughly the same expected performance. An alpha-enabling transaction might consist of selling one emerging market fund and investing the equivalent amount of money in a different fund. Last year, such a transaction could have generated a loss in the range of 30 percent, which could have been used to offset gains from U.S. equities. Once again, a transaction that, by itself, does nothing for the portfolio can enable a manager to undertake another transaction that would not be feasible because of taxes.

These two examples illustrate the fact that alpha enabling is not limited by asset class or type of security. For example, the same type of transaction can be developed for a bond portfolio. Anyone who is holding a capital loss in a bond portfolio can sell a AAA rated municipal bond to buy another AAA rated municipal bond.

After-Tax Performance Evaluation

James M. Poterba[1]
Mitsui Professor of Economics
Massachusetts Institute of Technology

Focusing on after-tax returns is a great way to add value and gain competitive advantage in the investment management business. Managers need to understand the factors that affect tax efficiency, to realize that a "one size fits all" performance measure and tax strategy will not work, and to integrate portfolio management with income tax and estate tax planning. Algorithms, such as the "accrual equivalent" tax rate, can help managers educate clients about the various implications of taxes for their portfolios.

The after-tax return associated with a given pretax return may vary considerably among individual tax-paying clients. Portfolio returns from the perspective of pretax reporting or performance management for tax-exempt clients can look very different from returns from the perspective of tax-paying individual investors.

This presentation focuses on the general issue of measuring after-tax performance—how taxes interact with performance management. This focus includes the AIMR Performance Presentation Standards (AIMR-PPS™ standards) and, more generally, the design of broad-based performance evaluation standards. This presentation examines whether an algorithm can be designed and used to tell a particular client the likely after-tax consequences of various portfolio strategies and to compare the after-tax performance of various managers. The presentation also provides an overview of the U.S. income tax environment for high-net-worth households, with particular emphasis on capital gains tax issues. Finally, the presentation reviews three important estate-planning tools that individuals can use to effectively manage estate taxes.

Why the After-Tax Focus

A focus on after-tax returns is worthwhile for several reasons. One is that most managers who work with individual clients know that increasingly sophisticated individual investors are demanding analysis of how their taxes are influenced by manager behavior, portfolio selection, and asset allocation. Therefore,

managers need to report results in a way that puts taxes into the broader picture.

Another reason is that reducing the tax drag on a portfolio may be an easier way of increasing after-tax returns than searching for additional pretax risk-adjusted returns (alpha). For example, when a manager is liquidating a position, selling highest-cost-basis shares rather than shares with an acquisition price close to the average basis is straightforward and enhances after-tax returns. A manager does not need to be a rocket scientist or need to accurately predict future earnings to follow that strategy. Therefore, a focus on after-tax returns allows recognition that there is some "low-hanging fruit" that many managers can harvest.

Finally, being able to make a coherent presentation on the tax consequences of various investment strategies and management styles can gain a manager an advantage in the competition for client money.

Factors Affecting Tax Efficiency

Certain key factors influence any portfolio's tax efficiency—that is, the difference between the portfolio's pretax return and its after-tax return for a taxable investor:

- *Portfolio turnover.* Portfolio turnover is clearly one of the key factors affecting tax efficiency, but the notion that high turnover equals bad tax efficiency is a myth. Turnover is like cholesterol: There is good, and there is bad. Good turnover is the harvesting of losses and the early realization of positions that have losses. Bad turnover is the selling of gains and the early triggering of capital gains tax liability. Tax-efficient portfolios should have more of the good and less of the bad turnover.

[1]This presentation is reprinted from the AIMR proceedings *Investment Counseling for Private Clients* (Charlottesville, VA: AIMR, 1999).

- *Inflows versus withdrawals.* A second key factor affecting tax efficiency is the pattern of asset inflows and withdrawals. The importance of this factor is particularly clear when examining the after-tax return performance of mutual funds. Consider two funds that are holding identical portfolios at the beginning of a year, and assume that these portfolios have substantial embedded, unrealized capital gains. One of the funds experiences large redemptions; the other experiences inflows during the year. The redeeming fund will have, on average, a higher tax burden for the year. A central issue that the AIMR-PPS Implementation Committee has wrestled with is the extent to which the manager is burdened with the taxes that are realized as a result of withdrawals that are beyond his or her control.

- *Dividend yield versus capital gains.* This factor, as most managers of taxable assets know, is critical. Because dividends are taxed more heavily than realized capital gains for most taxable investors and because unrealized capital gains are taxed even more favorably, a portfolio that generates a high fraction of its returns in the form of dividends will face a higher tax burden than a fund that generates primarily capital gains.

The factors driving tax efficiency are fairly simple, so clients might expect most managers to behave in a tax-efficient manner. But many managers do not. Several hypothetical examples will show how these factors can increase the difference between pretax and after-tax returns.

Mutual Fund Example. Suppose a hypothetical portfolio has the following characteristics:

Beginning-of-period market value	$10.00
Realized long-term capital gains	1.75
Realized short-term capital gains	0.25
Dividend income	0.50
Unrealized capital gains	0.50
Total pretax earnings	3.00

Pretax returns for this portfolio are an impressive 30 percent for the period. Unfortunately, after-tax returns are significantly less. After-tax returns on this fund, for an individual investor in the top U.S. federal marginal income tax bracket, can be calculated as follows:

$$\frac{\$1.75(1.00 - 0.20) + (\$0.25 + \$0.50)(1.00 - 0.396) + \$0.50}{\$10.00} = 23.5\%.$$

The terms $(1.00 - 0.20)$ and $(1.00 - 0.396)$ correspond, respectively, to the *after-tax* value of one dollar of realized long-term capital gains (taxed at 20 percent) and one dollar of realized short-term gains and dividend income, which is taxed at the federal marginal tax rate of 39.6 percent. Published estimates of pretax and after-tax returns on various mutual funds, such as those reported each year in *BusinessWeek*,

show just how much of the pretax return can be consumed by taxes. There is typically enormous variation among mutual fund managers in the amount of taxable income they generate for a given amount of pretax return. This variation reflects differences in each of the portfolio attributes described previously in this section.

Given the range of effective tax burdens among mutual funds and the diversity of effective tax rates among private clients, taxable investors should consider after-tax returns when selecting mutual funds.

Client Portfolio with Cash Withdrawals. Cash inflows and withdrawals also influence after-tax portfolio returns. The following example illustrates the measurement of after-tax performance for a client portfolio that has cash withdrawals:

Initial portfolio value	$1,000
Initial unrealized gains	500
Final prewithdrawal portfolio value	1,150
Final postwithdrawal portfolio value	1,100
Total capital appreciation	150
Client cash withdrawal	50
Realized long-term gains	140
Final unrealized gains	510
Cash dividends (distributed)	30

The pretax return on this portfolio is given by

$$\text{Pretax return} = \frac{\begin{array}{l}\text{Dividends}\\ + \text{ Change in portfolio value}\\ + \text{ Cash withdrawal}\end{array}}{\text{Initial value}}.$$

In this example, the pretax return is 18 percent. Suppose the general AIMR-PPS algorithm for after-tax performance measurement is used to measure the after-tax returns. This algorithm is as follows:

$$\text{After-tax return} = \frac{\begin{array}{l}\text{Realized long-term gains } (1 - t_{CG})\\ + (\text{Realized short-term gains}\\ + \text{ Dividends}) \,(1 - t_{DIV})\\ + \text{ Unrealized gains} + \text{Tax-free income}\\ + \text{ Client withdrawal adjustment factor}\end{array}}{\text{Starting asset value}},$$

where t_{CG} stands for the marginal tax rate on long-term capital gains realizations and t_{DIV} stands for the ordinary income tax rate that applies to dividend income. These tax rates are set at 20 percent and 39.6 percent, respectively.

In this algorithm, the client withdrawal adjustment factor is

$$\frac{t_{CG}(\text{Net withdrawal})(\text{Realized} + \text{Unrealized gains})}{(\text{Final portfolio value} + \text{Net withdrawal})}.$$

When the AIMR-PPS algorithm is used, the after-tax return is significantly less—14.58 percent—than the pretax return of 18 percent. The client withdrawal factor *raises* the reported after-tax return by 6 basis points.

Measuring After-Tax Performance

Differences in investors' income tax rates, and the interplay between investor characteristics and decisions about realizing capital gains, represent major challenges to measuring and evaluating after-tax performance. Therefore, managers need to understand how each investor's federal tax rates and potential estate taxes interact to influence portfolio management decisions. A good starting point for this analysis is the AIMR-PPS algorithm for measuring after-tax performance.

AIMR-PPS Algorithm. According to the AIMR-PPS standards, managers are to use the maximum federal statutory rate for each type of client. So, a manager would use 20 percent as the statutory long-term capital gains rate. But the tax rates clients face actually can vary, even among high-net-worth clients. Therefore, managers may want to customize this rate in the calculation of after-tax return. An investor with large capital loss carryforwards from a failed past investment may face a lower effective capital gains tax rate than someone without such a loss carryforward.

The AIMR-PPS standards also tell managers to exclude state and local taxes. The argument for doing so is that people live in different states. Everyone lives in some state, however, and for people who live in high-tax-burden states—in California (where the top income tax rate is 11 percent), New York (where the rate is 7–8 percent at the state level and more for New York City), and Massachusetts (which used to have a 12 percent tax rate on interest and dividend income)—managers should include the state tax rate in the algorithm so they can report what those taxes do to their clients' returns. Few investors would try to compare the returns on taxable and tax-exempt bond portfolios without recognizing the role of federal and state taxes. Similarly, a manager needs to recognize the role of state and local taxes in after-tax equity portfolio performance.

Individual Federal Tax Rates. Individual investors' federal tax rates vary for several reasons.

■ *Dependence of taxes on income, not wealth.* Some investors have substantial accumulated net worth, but their incomes do not put them in the top end of the income distribution. Managers can get a more systematic handle on this information than from anecdotal client interviews from a database that is collected every three years by the U.S. Federal Reserve Board, which is summarized in the Survey of Consumer Finances. This survey is the best publicly available nonproprietary information on the highest-net-worth part of the U.S. population. In collecting these data, the Fed focuses on households in wealthy communities. The result is a database that includes a nontrivial number of respondents from the segment of the U.S. population with the highest net worth.

The data show that only about a fifth of the households that were in the top 1 percent of the income distribution in 1995 were also in the top 1 percent of the net-worth distribution. In 1995, a family needed an income of about $225,000 to be in the top 1 percent of the income distribution. To be in the top 1 percent of the net-worth group, a family needed about $3 million in total household assets, including retirement accounts.

Whether investment managers' clients have high net worth or high income or both may not be clear. Part of the reason is that many individuals in high-net-worth households are past their prime earning years; they may be retirees whose income is primarily capital income. At the same time, some high-earning younger households may not yet have had time to accumulate substantial assets.

■ *Variation in income and asset values.* Taxes also vary because different assets generate different income profiles. People with substantial net worth in real estate or municipal bonds, for example, may have low taxable income relative to others in their net-worth category. Therefore, their tax status may be different from that of others with similar net worth.

■ *Special circumstances.* Finally, individuals' taxes vary because of "specialized tax circumstances." The importance of particular tax conditions, such as tax-planning problems generated by low-cost-basis stock, the alternative minimum tax (AMT), or loss carryforwards, is hard to identify. Nevertheless, such factors generate substantial scope for variations in tax rates.

These issues argue against using a one-size-fits-all performance measure. Managers need to think about a particular client's circumstances. The differences can be accounted for in simple computer programs that allow one to plug in various marginal tax rates as well as underlying information about the realization of gains and the income components of a given pretax return. Once the manager understands the person's marginal federal and state tax rates and other tax complications, the manager can tailor the presentation to those conditions.

Marginal Income Tax Rates. The notion of the "effective marginal tax rate" rather than the "average tax burden" should drive both managers' and clients' behavior. In 1998, the top federal marginal tax rates on interest and dividends were 39.6 percent starting at $271,050 of taxable income, 36 percent starting at $151,750, and 31 percent starting at $99,600. In addition, phase-out rules on deductions can propel top-bracket taxpayers into a tax bracket with a marginal tax rate as high as 41 percent. Managers can get a handle on how the rules on deductions affect a client's marginal tax rate by asking the client to add another $200 of interest income to his or her reported taxable income and then to recompute the taxes. In many cases, this additional income will not change the taxes by 39.6 percent times $200. It will change the taxes by more in some (most!) cases and by less in others. This exercise will give managers an idea of the true marginal tax rate the client faces.

The actual dividend tax rate faced by households with different characteristics is revealing. **Table 1** is based on a data set that the U.S. Internal Revenue Service (IRS) has released for researchers that includes actual (but anonymous) tax returns for tax year 1994. Note that for households that reported at least $50,000 of dividend and interest income, only about 40 percent were facing tax rates higher than 37 percent. Many people who reported that much in dividend and interest income fell in the 28 percent bracket. In other words, a significant number of households with substantial liquid assets face a marginal tax rate that is lower than the top rate. In the category of households receiving dividends and interest of more than $200,000, about 70 percent faced tax rates of more than 37 percent, whereas nearly 95 percent of those who have high wage and salary income are in the 37–41 percent tax range. There is more variation in the taxes on capital income than on earned income.

Capital Gains Taxes. Taxes on interest and dividends are not a very exciting part of the after-tax portfolio problem. Capital gains are where the action is. Most managers know the tax rules on short-term versus long-term capital gains. The tax rate on short-term capital gains—gains on securities held for less than one year—can go as high as 39.6 percent. Today, the top rate on long-term capital gains is 20 percent; starting in 2005, that rate will come down to 18 percent on assets that have been held for at least five years. The difference between the rates on short-term and long-term gains will be even larger in the future

than it is today. The tax-efficient strategy, therefore, when all other aspects of a portfolio are the same, is to realize losses and hold gains until they become long term.

The advantages of generating long-term capital gains relative to other kinds of portfolio income are larger today than they have been in the past. **Table 2** shows how the Taxpayer Relief Act of 1997 increased the advantages of tax-efficient investing. As recently as 1989, the top marginal tax rate on the highest dividend income and interest income recipients was 28 percent, which was also the top tax rate on capital gains. During the past decade, a zero tax rate differential has widened to a 20 percentage point differential. In the future, the difference between taxes on capital income and long-term capital gains could be as large as 23 percentage points.

Table 2. Top Federal Marginal Tax Rate over Time

Category	1996	1998	2005 (estimate)
Dividends and interest	~41%	~41%	41%
Long-term capital gains	28	20	18

This tax environment explains the benefits of tax-efficient portfolio management, but it also raises the issue of tax code risk. The tax system can shift in ways that destroy the advantages of previous tax-efficient behavior. Should investors and managers try to hedge bets on the tax system? Should taxpayers hold some qualified money in a Roth Individual Retirement Account and some in a traditional IRA? The tax treatment of these accounts is different, and one (the Roth) is not affected by future changes in marginal income tax rates. The answer is probably yes, although deciding how to model tax code risk is an unexplored problem.

Unrealized Capital Gains. One of the most difficult problems in measuring after-tax portfolio performance concerns handling unrealized capital

Table 1. Percentage of Households Paying Various Marginal Federal Tax Rates

Marginal Tax Rate	Dividends + Interest > $50,000	Dividends + Interest > $200,000	Wages + Salaries > $500,000
< 16 percent	10.0%	10.5	1.0
16–29 percent	28.4	13.8	3.5
29–37 percent	22.7	4.1	0.3
37–41 percent	37.7	70.2	94.7
> 41 percent	1.3	1.6	0.6
Number of taxpayers	402,800	51,000	76,300

Source: Calculations made using National Bureau of Economic Research TAXSIM model.

gains. The AIMR-PPS standards recommend ignoring potential future taxes on unrealized capital gains. I believe that some positive tax burden should be applied to unrealized gains because they are not untaxed but, rather, carry a contingent future tax liability.

The precise tax burden on unrealized gains depends on client circumstances. First, is the client likely to face substantial "forced realizations"? Such realizations may result from a transaction that sells them out involuntarily from a position in a low-cost-basis stock or from a substantial consumption demand on the client's part—demand for a new house, a new yacht, or so on. Second, is the client someone who, perhaps because of age, is in a position, from the standpoint of dynastic wealth accumulation, to take advantage of basis step-up at death? Third, is the client going to carry out a gifting strategy that will transfer asset basis to the next generation? If so, the manager should consider carryover basis rather than basis step-up as the likely scenario for assets received by the next generation. These issues can be explored with clients to determine what capital gains tax circumstances apply. They need to be covered in the client's investment plan, not left to the tax planners.

One way to describe the capital gains burden on unrealized gains is with the "accrual equivalent" capital gains tax rate. This concept finds the accrual tax system that gives the client the same total after-tax portfolio value at the end of the "realization period" as the current realization-based system, assuming asset sale at the end of the realization period. The approach is similar to asking what tax rate in New Zealand (which uses an accrual system on capital gains) would give you the same wealth after tax at the end of a given number of years as the 20 percent realization-based tax rate in the United States. The concept is useful to managers in explaining that deferring taxes is not the same as never paying them. It is a way of quantifying the interest-free loan a client is getting from the IRS when the client defers realizing capital gains on a position.

For example, suppose a client buys an asset in Year 0 for $100 and it generates capital gains at 10 percent a year. The asset pays no dividends. If the gains were realized each year and taxed as short-term gains (that is, every 364 days, the manager realized the gains on the position), then the after-tax return each year would be

$$10(1.00 - 0.396) = 6.04\%$$

because the short-term capital gains tax rate is 39.6 percent. After 10 years, no additional taxes would be due and the value would be

$$\$100.00(1.064)^{10} = \$185.96.$$

The value of the portfolio would be greater if the asset were held for 10 years and then the capital gains were realized. Assuming that the asset grew at 10 percent a year for 10 years and that 20 percent of the gains were taxed away in Year 10, the asset's after-tax value in 10 years would be

$$(1.00 - 0.20)[\$100.00(1.10)^{10} - \$100.00] + \$100.00 = \$227.50.$$

The accrual equivalent tax rate depends on the rate of return the asset manager would have had to earn on an after-tax basis year after year to get to the value of $227.50 in 10 years. To find this key bit of information, simply solve the following expression for R, the rate of return:

$$\$100.00(1.00 + R)^{10} = \$227.50.$$

The answer is $R = 8.57\%$. Thus, the accrual equivalent tax rate is

$$\frac{10.00\% - 8.57\%}{10.00\%} = 0.143, \text{ or } 14.30\%.$$

Using the accrual equivalent rate is like comparing the accumulated assets in an IRA with assets that are invested in a taxable account. How can one compare the values of those two investments? One way would be to find the internal rate of return on assets in the IRA that provides the same return as that available, after tax, outside the IRA. The accrual equivalent tax rate is the tax rate that if it were charged to your account every year on the accruing gains, would give you the same after-tax portfolio value at the end of the planning horizon that you would have had if you had been working under the realization-based system in which you pay taxes only at the end. The 14.3 percent accrual equivalent tax rate can be compared with the other tax rates applicable to the client. Because clients are accustomed to thinking in terms of 39.6 percent as an interest tax burden and 20 percent as the statutory tax burden on long-term realized gains, the 14.3 percent is a comparable measure. It describes what the rate would have to be if every year the assets with unrealized gains were marked to market and taxed on their gains.

The accrual equivalent tax rate provides a flexible tool for analyzing future tax burdens. If the client's tax rate is likely to change in the future, the manager can build that change into the calculation of an accrual equivalent tax rate. It can also be used to illustrate the value of deferring capital gains realizations over different horizon lengths.

Table 3 shows how the accrual equivalent tax rate changes as the holding period increases. If capital gains were realized after one year, the after-tax return would be 8 percent, which implies a 20 percent effective tax burden relative to the pretax 10 percent return. By 20 years, the tax burden is down to about 10 percent. The best outcome, as far as taxes go, is if

After-Tax Performance Evaluation

Table 3. Accrual Equivalent Return by Holding Period

Holding Period	Return
1 year	8.00%
5 years	8.28
10 years	8.57
20 years	8.98
Until death	10.00

the asset is held until death because then the tax liability is extinguished. If this asset generates only capital gains, the accrual equivalent return moves up to the 10 percent pretax return because of basis step-up at death.

The tax return data the IRS receives indicate that in the mid-1990s, the average holding period for corporate stock on which gains were subject to long-term capital gains tax treatment was about 6.5 years. Managers may be able to persuade their clients to hold assets longer by using a similar analysis to that of Table 3. This table can also illustrate the important benefits of a low-realization tax-management strategy.

Estate Tax Issues. Table 3 shows the potentially substantial tax savings that can flow from holding appreciated assets until death. Is the scenario realistic? Managers need to make some assumptions about the future tax circumstances of clients and about their estate-planning advice to evaluate the chance of basis step-up.

Life expectancy is one factor that applies in judging the likelihood of holding an asset until death. **Table 4** shows that life expectancy in the United States is quite long, even for people already at advanced ages. These data are based on the entire U.S. population, and the wealthy clients with whom managers deal are likely to live longer than these averages. The exact cause of wealth-related differences in mortality experience is not known, but there is a stark disparity between the mortality rates faced by those

Table 4. Life Expectancy at Various Ages, 1994

Age/Sex	Years Expectancy
65-year old	
Man	16.1
Woman	20.0
75-year old	
Man	9.8
Woman	12.8
85-year old	
Man	5.3
Woman	6.9

Source: U.S. Social Security Administration, unpublished tables used in preparing the 1995 Social Security Administration Trustee's Report.

in the bottom 20 percent of household income or wealth distribution and those at the top. In short, even if the client is an 85-year-old woman, the client's life expectancy may be 7 years, so whether a basis step-up is just around the corner is hard to judge. Managers, therefore, need to be mindful that the planning horizon, even for older clients, could be substantial.

Most decedents with substantial estates die at quite advanced ages. **Table 5** shows that in 1992, nearly two-thirds of taxable decedents were in their 80s when they died and more than three-quarters of the value of the estates reported were for decedents who were older than 70.

Table 5. Age Distribution of 1992 Taxable Decedents

Age at Death (years)	Percentage of Tax Returns	Percentage of Estate Value
< 50	1.9%	3.1%
50–60	3.1	6.2
60–70	9.9	16.0
70–80	23.4	26.7
> 80	61.7	47.9

Source: Martha B. Eller, "Federal Taxation of Wealth Transfers, 1992–1995," *Statistics of Income Bulletin* (Winter 1996–97):8–63.

The estate tax is a large and important tax in relation to other taxes for the small set of taxpayers who are likely to face it. The estate tax will change in the future as a result of a sliding scale of tax thresholds that will phase in between now and 2006. At the moment, an estate must be more than $625,000 to incur federal estate taxes; by 2006, the threshold will be $1 million. Today, marginal estate tax rates start at 37 percent at that $625,000 level and go as high as 60 percent. For a client who is thinking about keeping the assets that he or she has built for the next generation, the estate tax is thus an important part of the tax environment.

■ *Traditional bequests.* Assets can be passed from the wealth accumulator to the next generation in three ways, and the three methods have different tax consequences. The first method, and the one that receives the most attention, is traditional bequests. Assets are held until the accumulator, or the spouse of the accumulator, dies, and then the assets pass as a bequest to the next generation. Such assets are subject to the estate tax. They receive a basis step-up on any accrued unrealized capital gains, but the heirs face a variety of costs at the time of death, which may involve probate, valuation, and other issues. The costs are likely to be lower for publicly traded securities than for interests in privately held businesses or other, less liquid, assets.

©2000, Association for Investment Management and Research 63

■ *Tax-free* inter vivos *gifts.* The second way to transfer assets is by carrying out a gifting strategy during the lifetime of the accumulator generation. The allowed annual gifts of $10,000 per recipient per donor avoid the estate tax but do not participate in any step-up in basis, so the capital gains tax liability is not extinguished. In general, high-net-worth clients can have either capital gains tax relief or estate tax relief but not both. So, for taxpayers who could shift a substantial share of the wealth to the next generation in the form of *inter vivos* gifts, the tax gains from basis step-up are not as great as the simple analysis suggests. Capital gains taxes may be reduced at the cost of higher estate taxes.

For anyone who focuses on tax planning, the data on participation in gifting is remarkable. **Table 6** shows the percentage of households with household-ers 55 years old or older that gave assets of $10,000 in support of other households by net worth and by age. (The $10,000 is not $10,000 per child; it is simply giving $10,000 total.) The Survey of Consumer Finances, from which these data are drawn, asks donors about their gifts. It also asks the potential recipients, younger households typically, about the *inter vivos* gift amounts that they received. It turns out that the amount of *inter vivos* giving reported is about twice the amount of *inter vivos* receiving that is reported. No one understands why, but keep it in mind when ana-lyzing these numbers. Table 6 indicates that only about a fifth of the households that are headed by somebody over the age of 75 with a net worth of more than $2.5 million are making these kinds of gifts. Whatever the reason, the high-net-worth band is leav-ing unnecessary tax burdens to their heirs by underus-ing the *inter vivos* giving option.

Table 6. Households Making Gifts of at Least $10,000 a Year, 1995

Household Head's Age (years)	Net Worth $1.2 Million to $2.4 Million	Net Worth Greater than $2.4 Million
55–64	12%	29%
65–74	20	30
75+	26	22

Source: Federal Reserve Board, the Survey of Consumer Finances.

■ *Taxable gifts.* The third possibility, which is attractive only for very high-net-worth clients, is to make taxable gifts of more than the untaxed $10,000 per recipient a year. On an after-tax basis, pursuing a taxable gifting strategy is attractive for two reasons. The first is that the effective tax burden on a taxable gift is lower than the effective tax burden on a

bequest. Estates and gifts are taxed ostensibly under the same tax rules because we have a unified estate and gift tax in the United States. However, gifts are taxed on a net-of-tax basis, whereas bequests are taxed on a gross basis. The result is that if the estate tax rate facing a potential decedent is T, the tax rate on the gifts is $T/(1+T)$ instead of T. With a 50 percent statutory tax rate, the tax rate on the gifts (0.5/1.5) effectively becomes a 33 percent rate instead of a 50 percent rate. This consideration is very important, and it is widely underappreciated.

Taxable gifting is greatly preferable to leaving assets to pass through a taxable estate. This is true because of the tax rate difference and because paying the gift tax avoids the later estate and gift tax liability on whatever subsequent appreciation occurs on the assets given away. Appreciation on the assets and income on the assets will accrue to the next genera-tion instead of to the donor generation. The gifting strategy raises, once again, the income tax versus estate tax trade-off. Taxable gifts reduce estate tax burdens, but they preclude taking advantage of cap-ital gains basis step-up at death.

Only a tax lawyer can advise on the trade-offs among estate, gift, and capital gains taxes, but a starting point is that estate and gift tax rates tend to be much higher than the long-term capital gains rate. Estate and gift taxes start at 37 percent and can go as high as 60 percent. So, avoiding the estate tax and paying the capital gains tax at a rate of 18–20 percent along the way is often the preferable strategy.

This issue crystallizes the importance of under-standing client-specific circumstances in measuring after-tax results. For example, the trade-off between capital gains and estate/gift taxes is moot for those who are perfectly happy to leave their assets to a charitable foundation; they have a different strategy for reducing estate taxes, a strategy in which the cap-ital gains tax liability is not important. For clients who wish to leave their assets to their children, however, reducing the combination of capital gains taxes and estate taxes is important.

Conclusion

Measurement of after-tax portfolio performance is a crucial undertaking for any manager with private clients, and the AIMR-PPS standards are an impor-tant systematic effort to bring the industry up to speed in presenting returns on an after-tax basis.

Taxes are complicated, however, for high-net-worth clients. Managers may find that the AIMR-PPS standards are too broad for reporting performance for particular clients. Managers may need to custom-ize the algorithm by client or client group to recog-nize particular tax circumstances. This customization may involve building in specific tax rates, future tax liabilities, and even intergenerational plans in terms of wealth accumulation and wealth transfers. Tools such as the accrual equivalent tax rate provide managers a straightforward way to explain to clients how important and how valuable deferring capital gains can be. Managers need to think about modeling the client's after-tax returns for various portfolios.

Managers also need to consider the implications of gifting behavior. Apparently, most high-net-worth couples are likely to pass along some assets at the death of the second-to-die spouse, and the estate tax is likely to affect their intergenerational transfers. This practice raises the probability that some assets will face a zero capital gains tax rate (through the basis step-up) and underscores the need to integrate the investment manager into the tax-planning and tax-management picture. In some cases, wealth accumulation must be viewed from the family rather than the individual perspective. Gift giving complicates the problem of measuring marginal tax rates for after-death performance evaluation.

A common misconception is that taxes and investments can be managed separately. But investment managers cannot expect to achieve the best possible after-tax returns if they handle only the portfolio side of a client's affairs and turn over other aspects to tax managers, accountants, or tax planners. These aspects are intertwined. Accountants cannot try to minimize taxes when they are given a pretax return stream as the outcome of what the portfolio manager has done. Two-way communication is necessary if the strategy is to leave the client the largest after-tax wealth possible.

Question and Answer Session

James M. Poterba

Question: How do you benchmark after-tax returns when the accrual equivalent tax rate is used?

Poterba: You have all the mechanics in the basic formula, where a zero tax rate is being applied to the unrealized component of capital gains. The only question is whether to use a positive tax rate. If you want to work with the accrual tax rate, the modification is to put in a 1 minus 10 percent or 1 minus 12 percent tax burden on the unrealized capital gains term. Operationally, after you've run through the calculation for a client and identified the holding period as 20 years, that calculation tells you that the effective accrual capital gains rate on a gain that accrues today is on the order of 10 percentage points. You would assign that rate when you calculated after-tax returns.

Question: Is it reasonable to assume that a client who withdraws 10 percent a year from the assets will have different after-tax performance from a client who adds 10 percent a year to the assets?

Poterba: Yes, the situation is similar to the cost basis of a mutual fund that is getting positive cash flows versus one with negative cash flows. The one with positive flows doesn't have to realize as many gains. A fund with a 10 percent negative cash flow will have to realize gains and will have lower after-tax returns. That outcome is as true for a separately managed account as it is for a mutual fund.

I would use effective accrual rates to cast light on the effect of withdrawals versus infusions. For example, consider a client who plans to withdraw 10 percent of the portfolio each year. That information tells you that the time horizon or the effective duration for which the money is going to be under management is significantly shorter than for someone who plans to contribute 10 percent of the portfolio value each year until he or she dies. What's driving the difference is that the person who is adding money year after year is getting much longer average interest-free loans on the unrealized capital gains. You would expect to see a substantial difference in the after-tax return performance of those two portfolios.

Of course, the portfolio manager would be wise to recognize that the strategies and the investments that are optimal for someone who plans to add 10 percent a year will not be the same as the strategies that are optimal for someone who is planning to withdraw 10 percent a year. The trade-offs between the tax savings for low-dividend securities generating capital gains and the potential risks or other costs that arise from tilting the portfolio in that direction will be very different for those two clients.

Question: Is after-tax performance useful or not, then, in measuring manager value?

Poterba: What's the alternative? Is it best to ignore the fact that there were tax consequences associated with realizations and not try to make corrections? Some sort of measurement of after-tax performance makes sense; AIMR introduced the adjustment factor to account for such differences in strategies, but comparability is still not perfect. If you are trying to make comparisons of after-tax performance among managers, what you'd really like to see is the kinds of accounts a manager is running that have withdrawal characteristics like the account you're bringing to the table. The ability to dissect a manager's accounts by client objectives is the sort of information that could be useful, but that sort of detailed performance analysis is virtually impossible.

Question: How does one deal with realized losses that must be carried forward to a future tax year? Are any adjustments made?

Poterba: One thing you can do, in the spirit of the effective accrual tax rate, if a client has a very simple portfolio position with a limited number of managers working with the client and the client realizes a loss that is too large to use up this year (so the losses carry forward) is to ask: What is the discounted present value today of being able to reduce taxable income by $3,000 a year this year, next year, and all along the way until the loss is used up? If the tax rate at which you're deducting those losses is 39.6 percent today and you have $6,000 worth of losses, then you're getting 39.6 percent on the first $3,000 and 39.6 discounted for one period; so, it may be effectively 36 percent on next year's losses in today's dollars.

Simple analysis, however, omits the fact that managers can also modify their behavior with respect to future gain realizations so as to accelerate the use of the loss as a device for sheltering other gains. Therefore, the real issue is how valuable it is to have losses on the books today, given that the client can use these losses to realize some gains tax free and thereby rebalance the portfolio.

Question: What do you do about taking over a portfolio that has large embedded gains when you have been hired to diversify the portfolio (so, the after-tax returns are going to be biased downward)?

Poterba: You need to make some sort of correction in reporting portfolio performance, perhaps group client portfolios that start from similar positions. The issue is reminiscent of the debate that sometimes goes on in the popular press about mutual funds with different amounts of embedded capital gains: If you started tracking two funds today—one a new fund and the other an old fund with substantial embedded capital gains—you would expect the fund with the embedded capital gains to generate more taxable realizations going forward. Comparing the managers would be unfair because they start from different positions.

Question: At what net worth should you suggest to someone that they gift? For example, is $1.2 million enough assets for a 70-year-old couple that may face nursing home costs?

Poterba: The most likely explanation for the low level of taxable gifting, at least among those with net worth below, say, $3 million, is the fear of substantial expenses sometime before the end of their lives. Nursing homes probably loom largest in those anxieties. In most case, those expenses do not, however, make a substantial dent in high-net-worth household assets. Something like 20 percent of 70-year-olds will go into a nursing home at some point before death—the percentage is higher for women than for men. Most stays in nursing homes are relatively short, although most of the dollars spent on nursing home care are spent for the small subset of very long-term stays. Most of these households retain substantial assets at the time of death of the surviving spouse. The reason I focused on the $2.5 million net-worth category is that in that range, potential nursing home bills will not draw down most of the accumulated assets.

One could probably build a simple Monte Carlo simulation to get a handle on the risk of nursing home need versus tax savings. For example, you could find out the rough odds of various expenditures and then point out the trade-off between, say, a 5 percent chance of needing to pay an expense and the saving of 40 percent in terms of the difference between the estate tax and the capital gains tax.

Combining Estate Planning with Asset Allocation

Gregory R. Friedman
Principal
Windermere Investment Associates, Inc.

Although estate planning has long played a critical role in preserving wealth for future generations, this area has been dominated by attorneys and trust administrators. Investment professionals, however, can benefit their clients by developing an understanding of how the mechanics of wealth-transfer techniques work. The integration of asset allocation techniques with estate-planning structures allows investment advisors to enhance the after-tax, multigenerational value of clients' overall portfolios.

This presentation examines the importance of integrating asset allocation techniques with several commonly used financial estate-planning vehicles. The first portion of this presentation focuses on describing the mechanics of two specific trust vehicles designed to reduce taxes. The final section considers the important and beneficial effect that funding these trust vehicles with the right kinds of investments can have on maximizing multigenerational wealth transfer.

Gifts, Charity, and Taxes

Clients are often confused and even paralyzed by the sheer number of decisions they are asked to make regarding investment strategies, financial planning advice, and tax issues. Nevertheless, when investment advisors peel back the jargon and focus clients on their fundamental attitudes about wealth, the investment decision-making process becomes more straightforward. Stated simply, investors can do only so many things with their wealth. First and foremost, clients can spend it. In this presentation, spending does not mean buying a yacht or a home or jewelry; such spending is simply reinvesting in nonfinancial assets, which is an asset allocation decision. True spending means consumption—in other words, buying things a person can eat, smoke, or wear.

For most wealthy individuals, their investment portfolios are likely to be larger than the amount that can be consumed. Such clients possess only three remaining options for their money: They can give it to their children, donate it to charity, or pay it in taxes.

Individuals have differing objectives. Some want to pass as much wealth as they can to their children, and others worry about spoiling them. Some are charitable; others are selfish. Many clients have not yet decided what they want to achieve with their wealth, so they feel uncertain about irrevocably committing to a plan of personal spending versus wealth transfer versus charitable giving. The only characteristic shared by nearly every client is that no one wants to pay taxes.

Given the near universal aversion to the payment of taxes, the financial and legal communities have developed a series of clever techniques designed to minimize such payments. The two commonly employed methods are the charitable remainder unit trust (CRUT) and the grantor retained annuity trust (GRAT).

Charitable Remainder Unit Trust. A CRUT enables individuals to transfer assets to an irrevocable trust that is structured both to make an annual cash flow distribution back to them during their lifetime and to transfer the remaining assets to charity upon their death.

A client who establishes a CRUT benefits in a number of ways. First, the transfer of assets defers (or eliminates) the capital gains taxes associated with the sale of the low-cost assets. Second, the transfer creates a charitable tax deduction, which can provide a tax shelter for income or capital gains in the main portfolio. Third, the transfer generates an annual cash flow distribution back to the main portfolio. This cash flow establishes annual liquidity, and clients psychologically view the distributions from the CRUT as income. (Of course, clients can sell low-cost assets in their main portfolio and create liquidity for themselves, but most are reluctant to do so.) Finally, at the termination of the CRUT, the residual wealth transfers to charity, which satisfies the client's charitable intent.

Individuals interested purely in charity would not engage in a CRUT transaction but would instead make direct and current charitable gifts. The purpose of a CRUT, however, is to retain some benefit from the value of the assets gifted. Ultimately, either at the end of the CRUT's term or at the end of the grantor's life, the assets remaining in the CRUT pass to charity.

Grantor Retained Annuity Trust. In broad terms, a GRAT has the same general objective as a CRUT: to transfer assets from an individual's portfolio to a trust in a way that minimizes or eliminates taxes.

As with a CRUT, the grantor (the individual funding the GRAT) derives a direct economic benefit from the arrangement because the GRAT pays an annuity back to his or her main portfolio. At the end of the GRAT's term, assets remaining in the trust after satisfying the required annual annuity payments are transferred to the next generation free of the 55 percent gift and estate tax.

Case Study

As an example of the role of the complex considerations involved in using irrevocable trusts, consider a hypothetical client, I.M. Rich, who recently sold his Silicon Valley firm Mystock.com to Fertilizer Company for $100 million in Fertilizer Company common stock. The managers of Fertilizer Company view Mystock.com as an attractive means of diversifying the company's revenue stream and believe that the acquisition offers potential synergies with its existing business. Rich, however, is skeptical about Fertilizer Company's wisdom because it paid him $100 million for his company, which has little to no prospect of generating positive earnings. Instead of holding onto Fertilizer Company shares and hoping for future appreciation, Rich decides to sell. Not surprisingly, Rich is soon barraged by numerous phone calls from insurance agents, estate planners, and other investment professionals seeking to offer their "advice."

Although the sheer variety of investment options confuses Rich, who is unfamiliar with the investment arena, he is resolute about his life's objectives. He wants to maximize the transfer of his wealth to his children—subject to gifting $38 million to charity—but only at his death. He wants to maintain the lifestyle to which he has become accustomed, which requires $1 million in annual after-tax income.

Finally, because he might decide that his children are not deserving or because he might choose to start another company or simply change his priorities, he wants no more than 25 percent of the portfolio to be dedicated to irrevocable transactions. He expects his investment time horizon, or life expectancy, to be 20 years, and he is in the top income-tax bracket.

Rich first wants to know how much his three children would receive if he simply sold his Fertilizer Company shares, paid the required capital gains tax, and reinvested the proceeds in a diversified portfolio. The first step is to assess Rich's tolerance for risk and to develop an appropriate asset allocation plan. **Table 1** shows the assumptions used to design an efficient portfolio suitable for Rich's risk tolerance. In this simple example, Rich is presented with three asset classes that represent alternate levels of risk: low for bonds, moderate for U.S. stocks, and very high for emerging market stocks.

Table 1. Asset Class Assumptions

Asset Class	Pretax Total Return	Capital Appreciation	Yield	Risk
Bonds (tax free)	5.0%	0.0%	5.0%	5.5%
Bonds (taxable)	7.0	0.0	7.0	5.5
U.S. stocks	8.5	6.5	2.0	14.0
Emerging market stocks	12.0	11.0	1.0	27.0

After reviewing his tolerance for risk, Rich selects a portfolio composed of 40 percent bonds, 45 percent U.S. equities, and 15 percent emerging market stocks. As shown in **Table 2**, if Rich sold his $100 million in stock, paid the capital gains tax, and reinvested in this diversified portfolio, the portfolio—by the end of Year 1—would generate investment income of about $3 million and would appreciate by about $4.5 million. Offsetting these sources of return, Rich would have to pay management fees of about $400,000 and income tax of about $308,000 (because of the dividends generated by the stocks). Also, because of the active management of U.S. large-cap and emerging market stocks, Rich would incur short-term capital gains taxes of about $51,000 and long-term capital gains taxes of about $150,000. Finally, Rich would pay a whopping $20 million of taxes associated with the liquidation of the zero-cost stock in Fertilizer Company. All told, at the end of Year 1, Rich's main portfolio would be worth $85.6 million (nearly $15 million less than what he started with).

From Rich's perspective, the most important consideration is not the value of the portfolio after only one year but rather the expected value of the portfolio in 20 years—the end of his expected

Table 2. After-Tax Annual and Terminal Wealth for Portfolio Using No Financial Planning

	Year 1	Year 2	Year 20
Starting balance	$100,000,000	$85,638,918	$222,602,478
Annual spending	–1,000,000	–1,000,000	–1,000,000
Investment income	3,019,500	2,581,487	5,630,376
Capital gains	4,529,249	3,854,393	9,445,563
Management fees	–398,475	–340,672	–743,025
Income taxes	–308,731	–263,946	–575,683
Short-term gains taxes (active management)	–51,749	–68,157	—
Long-term gains taxes (active management)	–150,876	–211,520	—
Short-term gains taxes (rebalancing)	—	–17,837	—
Long-term gains taxes (rebalancing)	–20,000,000	–141,127	—
Estate tax	—	—	–106,176,423
Charitable gift	—	—	–38,000,000
Ending balance	$ 85,638,918	$90,049,376	$ 91,183,286

lifespan. Of particular importance is the amount that would remain for his children after the desired $38 million distribution to charity and the required payment of the 55 percent estate tax. By the end of his life, on an after-tax, preliquidated basis, Rich's portfolio would have grown to almost $223 million. Upon Rich's death, the executor of his estate would transfer $38 million to charity in order to satisfy Rich's stated charitable objectives. The remaining assets in the portfolio would be taxed at 55 percent, resulting in an estate tax bill of about $106 million. After all transfers, taxes, and fees are paid, the children would receive $91.18 million. This amount represents the projected value of the portfolio absent any type of estate planning. Any other strategies must transfer greater wealth to Rich's children than this amount in order for them to be considered.

To understand how devastating fees and taxes can be, consider the fact that 56 percent of Rich's portfolio would be consumed by the following costs: taxes from rebalancing the portfolio, 7 percent; management fees, 4 percent; income tax, 3 percent; estate tax, 37 percent; and manager-generated taxes, 5 percent. Consequently, after Rich's gift to charity (13 percent of his terminal wealth), the transfer of remaining wealth to the children would represent only 31 percent of the ending value of his portfolio.

The Value of Financial Planning. Rich's attorney has suggested that he consider funding a $25 million CRUT in order to defer some of the up-front tax payments associated with the liquidation of Fertilizer Company Stock. In order to isolate the value of the CRUT transaction, assume that the asset allocation within the CRUT is identical to the asset allocation within Rich's main portofolio (i.e., 40 percent bonds,

45 percent U.S. stock, and 15 percent emerging market stock). The CRUT offers three advantages. First, transferring $25 million to the CRUT would generate a 10 percent, or $2.5 million, charitable deduction that could be used to offset income or capital gains in Rich's main portfolio. Second, the CRUT would generate a projected cumulative cash flow of $35.4 million that would flow back into Rich's main portfolio. Third, income and realized capital gains generated within the CRUT would not be subject to tax until distributed. The assets remaining in the CRUT are projected to grow to $29 million by the end of I.M. Rich's life. This amount would flow directly to the charity but would be insufficient to meet his stated goal of a $38 million charitable contribution, so an additional $9 million must come from his testamentary estate. The remaining assets of $206 million would be taxed at 55 percent, leaving an estimated $92.8 million to go to Rich's children.

Thus, although the CRUT is principally a charitable vehicle, it can also add value for Rich's children by deferring the payment of capital gains tax on the low-cost Fertilizer Company shares transferred to the CRUT. Rich's baseline case (no planning) would transfer $91.18 million to his children, whereas a CRUT with identical asset allocation would generate $92.86 million—an added value of $1.68 million arising simply from the value of a financial planning vehicle.

The Value of Proper Asset Location. The allocation of assets in Rich's main portfolio and in the CRUT are identical. Rich's investment advisor recognizes that because these two entities are taxed in different ways, varying the types of investments placed in the CRUT may improve its effectiveness. Testing this assumption involves examining the impact that holding bonds in the CRUT would have on final wealth versus the impact that using aggressive assets would have. Note that in all scenarios examined, the aggregate asset allocation of Rich's combined portfolio (main account plus the CRUT) always remains at 40 percent bonds, 45 percent U.S. stocks and 15 percent emerging market stock. As shown in **Table 3**, aggressive investments are clearly the best alternative. The value of the CRUT itself, relative to using no financial planning at all, would be $1.7 million. Funding the CRUT with aggressive assets would increase the value Rich can transfer to his children by $8.35 million. Thus, proper asset allocation can add significantly greater value than the value of the CRUT vehicle itself.

A second strategy that has been suggested to Rich is to transfer $25 million to a 10-year GRAT. Like the CRUT, this strategy would generate cash flow back into Rich's main portfolio (a projected $30.7 million in this case). Unlike the CRUT, however, a GRAT would not result in the creation of a charitable deduction or in the deferral of capital gains taxes. Also, assets remaining in the GRAT at the end of its 10-year term need not be turned over to charity but instead could be transferred to Rich's children free of estate taxes. If the GRAT and the main portfolio share an identical asset allocation, at the end of the term, the GRAT would generate an additional value for Rich's children of $4.5 million relative to no financial planning. Under this set of assumptions, the GRAT is a more effective wealth transfer tool than the CRUT.

As with the CRUT transaction, varying the types of investments within the GRAT may improve the effectiveness of the strategy. As shown in **Table 4,** placing aggressive assets within the GRAT would generate a sizeable $22 million advantage over using no financial planning and approximately $18 million of additional value relative to a GRAT that has an allocation identical to the main portfolio. In short, proper asset allocation can generate a nearly fivefold increase in the value of the underlying financial planning strategy.

Finally, Rich wonders what would happen if he ignored all of these complex techniques and simply transferred a $25 million gift to his children today and paid the gift tax? As shown in **Table 5**, the combined ending value of Rich's portfolio and the children's portfolio totals $122 million. Compared with no financial planning, which would transfer about $91 million to the children, simply transferring a $25 million gift, paying the gift taxes today, and identically investing the two portfolios would add value of $31 million.

As with the other strategies examined in this presentation, varying the allocation of the aggressive and conservative assets for Rich's portfolio and his children's portfolio can add significant value. As shown in **Table 6**, loading the children's portfolio up with more aggressive investments would generate $49 million of additional value versus no planning and nearly $18 million more than with identical allocations. Again, note that for each type of allocation to the children's portfolio—identical, conservative, and aggressive—the risk profile of Rich's aggregate portfolio (that is, I.M. Rich's portfolio plus the children's) is the same.

Table 3. Effect of CRUT Asset Allocation on Wealth Transfer

	CRUT Allocation			Wealth Transfer to Children	Advantage over No CRUT
	Bonds	U.S. Stocks	Emerging Market Stocks		
No CRUT	0%	0%	0%	$91,183,286	—
Identically allocated CRUT	40	45	15	92,864,402	$1,681,116
Conservatively allocated CRUT	100	0	0	90,264,928	–918,358
Aggressively allocated CRUT	0	35	65	99,538,965	8,355,679

Table 4. Effect of GRAT Asset Allocation on Wealth Transfer

	GRAT Allocation			Wealth Transfer to Children	Advantage over No GRAT
	Bonds	U.S. Stocks	Emerging Market Stocks		
No GRAT	0%	0%	0%	$91,183,286	—
Identically allocated GRAT	40	45	15	95,661,874	4,478,588
Conservatively allocated GRAT	100	0	0	91,183,286	—
Aggressively allocated GRAT	0	35	65	113,230,328	22,047,042

Table 5. Total Wealth Transfer for Gifting Approach

	Year 1	Year 2	Year 2020
Main portfolio			
Starting balance	$100,000,000	$45,212,424	$ 84,534,364
Annual spending	–1,000,000	–1,000,000	–1,000,000
Gift to children	–25,000,000	—	—
Investment income	2,257,000	1,343,296	1,386,515
Capital gains	3,385,500	1,845,013	2,004,914
Fees and taxes	–20,680,076	–717,126	–324,740
Estate tax	–13,750,000	—	–26,146,603
Charitable gift	—	—	–38,000,000
Ending balance	$ 45,212,424	$46,683,607	$ 22,454,450
Children's portfolio			
Starting balance	$ 25,000,000	$26,661,681	$ 93,133,153
Investment income	762,500	817,572	2,868,617
Capital gains	1,143,750	1,370,301	5,222,772
Fees and taxes	–244,569	–301,947	–1,366,823
Ending balance	$ 26,661,681	$28,547,607	$ 99,857,719
Total Wealth Transfer	—	—	$122,312,169

Table 6. Effect of Asset Allocation on Children's Portfolio

	Children's Portfolio			Wealth Transfer to Children	Advantage over No Planning
	Bonds	U.S. Stocks	Emerging Market Stocks		
No planning	0%	0%	0%	$ 91,183,286	—
Identical children's portfolio	40	45	15	122,312,169	$31,128,883
Conservative children's portfolio	100	0	0	105,582,443	14,399,157
Aggressive children's portfolio	0	Varies[a]	Varies[a]	140,580,700	49,397,414

[a]In order to ensure that the portfolios (I.M. Rich's plus his children's) were, in the aggregate, always allocated 40 percent to bonds, 45 percent to U.S. stocks, and 15 percent to emerging market stocks, it was necessary to vary the allocation within the children's portfolio over time.

Conclusion

Estate taxes destroy multigenerational wealth. Preserving the value of a portfolio for two generations is difficult, and for three generations, nearly impossible. Financial planning can add substantial value, whether one chooses the simple option of transferring wealth to the children today or uses one of the more complex strategies, such as GRATs or CRUTs.

Proper asset allocation substantially increases the effectiveness of financial planning techniques. Investment professionals should gain a thorough understanding of the mechanics and tax characteristics of tax and estate planning vehicles and should allocate assets properly among them.

Question and Answer Session

Gregory R. Friedman

Question: How is the term of a GRAT determined?

Friedman: The term of a GRAT is at the discretion of the grantor and can range from the short term to 10 years or more. The longer the time frame, the lower the annual annuity payment that is required to zero out the implicit gift of the GRAT. The shorter the time frame, the higher the annuity payment that is required. GRATs typically have terms of from 5 to 10 years. Annual financing rate (AFR) factors published by the IRS make a 9-year time frame rather attractive.

Question: Why does allocating a segment of the portfolio, such as the children's assets, to higher-risk assets not increase the overall risk profile of the portfolio?

Friedman: Transferring $25 million to the children outright imposes a constraint on the asset allocation. In the aggregate, the children's portfolio and the main portfolio have a constant allocation of 40 percent bonds, 45 percent U.S. stocks, and 15 percent emerging market stocks. In isolation, the children's portfolio has a higher expected return and a higher standard deviation, but this increased risk is counterbalanced by I.M. Rich's portfolio, which has a lower expected return and a lower standard deviation. Being more aggressive makes sense for the children's portfolio. In this case, the risk profile is set to be the same for all portfolios. The differences in final wealth examined in this presentation are the result not of how much risk was taken but rather of where the aggressive versus the conservative investment assets were located.

Question: What are the tax advantages of a charitable lead trust (CLT)?

Friedman: The principal advantage of a CLT is that it generates a substantial charitable deduction that can provide a shelter from income tax or capital gains tax. The residual value of the proceeds (that is, the value remaining after the CLT has made its required annuity payments to charity) transfers to the next generation free of estate tax. So, the CLT is the reverse of the CRUT transaction, in which the residual amount flows to charity. A CLT and a GRAT have similar objectives. The idea is to fund the CLT with high-growth assets that will leave the trust with a high ending residual value. The CLT assets, however, need to be reasonably liquid because of the ongoing annuity payment to charity.

Question: If I.M. Rich had his $1 million distribution indexed to inflation, what would the consequences be?

Friedman: This example uses $1 million across the board for simplification, but as a practical matter, most of our clients ask us to model their expected spending to grow at the rate of inflation. Such an expectation would not have a material effect on the conclusions reached in this presentation.

Question: How do you determine risk tolerance, given differing objectives of the grantor?

Friedman: From a psychological standpoint, whether clients take on more or less risk in the aggregate depends on their personal risk tolerance. From a theo-retical standpoint, however, note that because I.M. Rich's claim on the portfolio represented only 6 percent of the portfolio, the children's tolerance for risk should govern the allocation of assets.

In working with clients, we will typically use examples similar to the ones described to illustrate not only the expected level of future wealth but also the worst-case scenarios. The choice to distribute wealth to the children today or to engage in a CRUT or a GRAT transaction should not be driven by the client's tolerance for risk. Certainly, the decision affects the taxation and the timing of the cash flows, but one can work through such problems analytically by using an after-tax asset allocation software program, such as Windermere Investment Associates' PORTAX. The techniques one employs—whether CRUTs, GRATs, or outright transfers—should not materially alter the aggregate portfolio's risk profile.

Question: Is the GRAT's advantage ($95.6 million transferred to the children versus $92.8 million transferred with the CRUT) caused by the fact that the taxes paid by the grantor are deductible for estate purposes, and what are the components of this added value?

Friedman: The principal advantage of a GRAT is the ability for I.M. Rich to transfer a portion of his assets out of his estate as opposed to leaving them in his portfolio and paying a 55 percent estate tax. The other difference is that in the CRUT transaction, distributions that come back into I.M. Rich's portfolio are taxable based on how those distributions were earned within the CRUT. If they were earned as ordinary income, he would pay taxes at a 39.6 percent rate. If they were earned as capital gains, he would pay 20 percent. Because a GRAT is considered to be "defective" for income-tax purposes, annuity payments made by the GRAT back to Rich are not considered to be taxable income for him. In this example, Rich could entirely avoid taxes on GRAT distributions by receiving payment of securities "in kind" instead of cash.

Question: If aggressive investment decisions turn out to have adverse results, will less wealth transfer at the end?

Friedman: Remember, in the examples described in this presentation, the asset allocation of Rich's aggregated portfolios remained the same, regardless of which financial planning strategy was used or how assets were apportioned among the strategies. In general, however, the answer to the question is that, yes, less wealth will be transferred if risky allocations are pursued and markets perform poorly.

Question: What is the rationale behind using emerging market stocks as a diversifying equity asset class rather than international stocks?

Friedman: International stocks are also a good diversifying asset class. During the 1990s, however, the correlation between international stocks and U.S. stocks began to converge. In fact, instead of evaluating international assets on the basis of the performance of the Europe/Australasia/Far East (EAFE) Index, if you look at the results of actual international managers, the correlation coefficients between international portfolios and U.S. portfolios are even higher. The examples in this presentation used emerging market stocks to provide a high-risk, high-return asset class that was materially different from U.S. stocks. The correlation coefficient of emerging market stocks has hovered at about 30–40 percent relative to U.S. equities, so they are a good diversifier (although they have not performed well recently). Over the long term, say 20 years, risk and return should again go hand in hand and emerging market stocks should post materially higher returns than U.S. equities.